OUR EXAGMINATION
ROUND HIS FACTIFICATION
FOR INCAMINATION
OF WORK IN PROGRESS

OUR EXAGMINATION ROUND HIS FACTIFICATION FOR INCAMINATION OF WORK IN PROGRESS

BY

Samuel Beckett, Marcel Brion, Frank Budgen,
Stuart Gilbert, Eugene Jolas, Victor Llona,
Robert McAlmon, Thomas McGreevy,
Elliot Paul, John Rodker, Robert Sage,
William Carlos Williams.

with

LETTERS OF PROTEST

BY

G. V. L. Slingsby and Vladimir Dixon.

FABER AND FABER
3 Queen Square
London

First published in 1929
by Shakespeare and Company, Paris
and by Faber and Faber Limited
Second impression 1961
First published in this edition 1972
Printed in Great Britain
by John Dickens & Co Ltd, Northampton
All rights reserved

ISBN 0 571 09925 4

TABLE OF CONTENTS

————

INTRODUCTION (1961)

The surviving authors of *Our Exagmination* have very kindly asked its former publisher to contribute to the re-issue of their work a few words about its origin. Many of the essays included were first published by Eugene Jolas in his review, *transition*: what, therefore, could be more fitting than an introduction by Mrs. Eugene Jolas ? But she has declined the honour, Mr. Stuart Gilbert has too, so it is left to me to tell how this little volume came about.

To begin with, I have a confession to make : when given a piece of *Work in Progress* to interpret by the author, I failed to pass my 'exagmination': whereas, as will be seen in the twelve essays in this volume, all these followers of the *Work* went around in it with the greatest ease.

'Our Exag', as at Shakespeare and Company it was called, is most valuable, indeed indispensable to readers of *Finnegans Wake* : they would do well to hear what these writers, friends and collaborators of Joyce, followers of his new work as it progressed, have to say on the subject. They had the advantage of hearing the hints that he would let fall and the delightful stories he told when in the company of his friends.

Our Exagmination is therefore unique. And it has the added charm of Joyce's presence, for Mr. Stuart Gilbert strongly suspects that Mr. Vladimir Dixon, author of 'A Litter', is James Joyce himself.

In 1929, date of publication of *Our Exagmination*, the future
Finnegans Wake was appearing in *transition* and its readers
were following it with excitement, though often losing their
way in the dark of this night piece.   They needed help :   the
articles contributed to *transition* by writers who had penetrated
deeply into the mysteries of *Work in Progress*, and other essays
on the subject, were assembled in the volume entitled (by
Joyce) *Our Exagmination round His Factification for In-
camination of Work in Progress*, and brought out by Shakespeare and Company.

Sylvia Beach.

DANTE... BRUNO. VICO.. JOYCE

BY

SAMUEL BECKETT

DANTE... BRUNO. VICO.. JOYCE

Samuel BECKETT.

The danger is in the neatness of identifications. The conception of Philosophy and Philology as a pair of nigger minstrels out of the Teatro dei Piccoli is soothing, like the contemplation of a carefully folded ham-sandwich. Giambattista Vico himself could not resist the attractiveness of such coincidence of gesture. He insisted on complete identification between the philosophical abstraction and the empirical illustration, thereby annulling the absolutism of each conception — hoisting the real unjustifiably clear of its dimensional limits, temporalising that which is extratemporal. And now here am I, with my handful of abstractions, among which notably : a mountain, the coincidence of contraries, the inevitability of cyclic evolution, a system of Poetics, and the prospect of self-extension in the world of Mr. Joyce's 'Work in Progress'. There is the temptation to treat every concept like 'a bass dropt neck fust in till a bung crate', and make a really tidy job of it. Unfortunately such an exactitude of application would imply distortion in one of two directions. Must we wring the neck of a certain system in order to stuff it into a contemporary pigeon-hole, or modify the dimensions of that pigeon-

4

hole for the satisfaction of the analogymongers? Literary criticism is not book-keeping.

. . . .

Giambattista Vico was a practical roundheaded Neapolitan. It pleases Croce to consider him as a mystic, essentially speculative, '*disdegnoso dell' empirismo*'. It is a surprising interpretation, seeing that more than three-fifths of his *Scienza Nuova* is concerned with empirical investigation. Croce opposes him to the reformative materialistic school of Ugo Grozio, and absolves him from the utilitarian preoccupations of Hobbes, Spinoza, Locke, Bayle and Machiavelli. All this cannot be swallowed without protest. Vico defines Providence as: '*una mente spesso diversa ed alle volte tutta contraria e sempre superiore ad essi fini particolari che essi uomini si avevano proposti; dei quali fini ristretti fatti mezzi per servire a fini più ampi, gli ha sempre adoperati per conservare l'umana generazione in questa terra*'. What could be more definitely utilitarianism? His treatment of the origin and functions of poetry, language and myth, as will appear later, is as far removed from the mystical as it is possible to imagine. For our immediate purpose, however, it matters little whether we consider him as a mystic or as a scientific investigator; but there are no two ways about considering him as an *innovator*. His division of the development of human society into three ages: Theocratic, Heroic, Human (civilized), with a corresponding classification of language: Hieroglyphic (sacred), Metaphorical (poetic), Philosophical (capable of abstraction and generalisation), was by no means new, although it must have appeared so to his contemporaries. He derived this convenient classification from the Egyptians, via Herodotus. At the same time it is impossible to deny the originality with which he applied and developed its implications. His exposition of the ineluctable circular progression of Society was completely new, although the germ of it was contained in Giordano Bruno's treatment of identified contraries. But it is in Book 2., described by himself as '*tutto il corpo... la chiave maestra... dell' opera*', that appears the unqualified originality of his mind; here he evolved a theory of the origins of poetry and language, the significance of myth, and the nature of barbaric civilization that must have appeared nothing less than an impertinent outrage against tradition. These two aspects of Vico have their reverberations, their reapplications — without however, receiving the faintest explicit illustration — in '*Work in Progress.*'

It is first necessary to condense the thesis of Vico, the scientific historian: In the beginning was the thunder: the thunder set free Religion, in its most objective and unphilosophical form — idolatrous animism: Religion produced Society, and the first social men were the cave-dwellers, taking refuge from a passionate Nature: this primitive family life receives its first impulse towards development from the arrival of terrified vagabonds: admitted, they are the first slaves: growing stronger, they exact agrarian concessions, and a despotism has evolved into a primitive feudalism: the cave becomes a city, and the feudal system a democracy: then an anarchy: this is corrected by a return to monarchy: the last stage is a tendency towards interdestruction: the nations are dispersed, and the Phoenix of Society arises out of their ashes. To this six-termed social progression corresponds a six-termed progression of human motives: necessity, utility, convenience, pleasure, luxury, abuse of luxury: and their incarnate manifestations: Polyphemus, Achilles, Caesar and Alexander, Tiberius, Caligula and Nero. At this point Vico applies

Bruno — though he takes very good care not to say so — and proceeds from rather arbitrary data to philosophical abstraction. There is no difference, says Bruno between the smallest possible chord and the smallest possible arc, no difference between the infinite circle and the straight line. The maxima and minima of particular contraries are one and indifferent. Minimal heat equals minimal cold. Consequently transmutations are circular. The principle (minimum) of one contrary takes its movement from the principle (maximum) of another. Therefore not only do the minima coincide with the minima, the maxima with the maxima, but the minima with the maxima in the succession of transmutations. Maximal speed is a state of rest. The maximum of corruption and the minimum of generation are identical: in principle, corruption is generation. And all things are ultimately identified with God, the universal monad, Monad of monads. From these considerations Vico evolved a Science and Philosophy of History, It may be an amusing exercise to take an historical figure, such as Scipio, and label him No. 3 ; it is of no ultimate importance. What is of ultimate importance is the recognition that the passage from Scipio to Caesar is as inevitable as the passage from Caesar to Tiberius, since the flowers of corruption in Scipio and Caesar are thé seeds of vitality in Caesar and Tiberius. Thus we have the spectacle of a human progression that depends for its movement on individuals, and which at the same time is independent of individuals in virtue of what appears to be a preordained cyclicism. It follows that History is neither to be considered as a formless structure, due exclusively to the achievements of individual agents, nor as possessing reality apart from and independent of them, accomplished behind their backs in spite of them, the work of some superior force, variously known as Fate, Chance, Fortune, God. Both

these views, the materialistic and the transcendental, Vico
rejects in favour of the rational. Individuality is the concre-
tion of universality, and every individual action is at the
same time superindividual. The individual and the universal cannot be considered as distinct from each other. History,
then, is not the result of Fate or Chance — in both cases the
individual would be separated from his product — but the
result of a Necessity that is not Fate, of a Liberty that is not
Chance (compare Dante's 'yoke of liberty'). This force he
called Divine Providence, with his tongue, one feels, very
much in his cheek. And it is to this Providence that we
must trace the three institutions common to every society :
Church, Marriage, Burial. This is not Bossuet's Providence,
transcendental and miraculous, but immanent and the stuff
itself of human life, working by natural means. Humanity
is its work in itself. God acts on her, but by means of her.
Humanity is divine, but no man is divine. This social and
historical classification is clearly adapted by Mr. Joyce as a
structural convenience — or inconvenience. His position is
in no way a philosophical one. It is the detached attitude of
Stephen Dedalus in 'Portrait of the Artist...' who describes
Epictetus to the Master of Studies as « an old gentleman
who said that the soul is very like a bucketful of water. »
The lamp is more important than the lamp-lighter. By structural I do not only mean a bold outward division, a bare skel-
eton for the housing of material. I mean the endless substan-
tial variations on these three beats, and interior intertwining
of these three themes into a decoration of arabesques — decoration and more than decoration. Part 1. is a mass of past
shadow, corresponding therefore to Vico's first human institution, Religion, or to his Theocratic age, or simply to an
abstraction — Birth. Part 2 is the lovegame of the children,

corresponding to the second institution, Marriage, or to the Heroic age, or to an abstraction — Maturity.   Part. 3. is passed in sleep, corresponding to the third institution, Burial, or to the Human age, or to an abstraction — Corruption.   Part 4 is the day beginning again, and corresponds to Vico's Providence, or to the transition from the Human to the Theocratic, or to an abstraction — Generation.   Mr. Joyce does not take birth for granted, as Vico seems to have done.   So much for the dry bones.   The consciousness that there is a great deal of the unborn infant in the lifeless octogenarian, and a great deal of both in the man at the apogee of his life's curve, removes all the stiff interexclusiveness that is often the danger in neat construction.   Corruption is not excluded from Part 1. nor maturity from Part 3.   The four 'lovedroyd curdinals' are presented on the same plane — 'his element curdinal numen and his enement curdinal marrying and his epulent curdinal weisswasch and his eminent curdinal Kay o' Kay !'   There are numerous references to Vico's four human institutions — Providence counting as one !   'A good clap, a fore wedding, a bad wake, tell hell's well' : ' their weatherings and their marryings and their buryings and their natural selections' : 'the lightning look, the birding cry, awe from the grave, everflowing on our times' : 'by four hands of forethought the first babe of reconcilement is laid in its last cradle of hume sweet hume'.

Apart from this emphasis on the tangible conveniences common to Humanity, we find frequent expressions of Vico's insistence on the inevitable character of every progression —or retrogression : 'The Vico road goes round and round to meet where terms begin.   Still onappealed to by the cycles and onappalled by the recoursers, we feel all serene, never you fret, as regards our dutyful cask.... before there was a man at all in

Ireland there was a lord at Lucan. We only wish everyone was as sure of anything in this watery world as we are of everything in the newlywet fellow that's bound to follow.....' 'The efferfreshpainted livy in beautific repose upon the silence of the dead from Pharoph the next first down to ramescheckles the last bust thing'. 'In fact, under the close eyes of the inspectors the traits featuring the chiaroscuro coalesce, their contrarieties eliminated, in one stable somebody similarly as by the providential warring of heartshaker with housebreaker and of dramdrinker against freethinker our social something bowls along bumpily, experiencing a jolting series of prearranged disappointments, down the long lane of (it's as semper as oxhousehumper) generations, more generations and still more generations' — this last a case of Mr. Joyce's rare subjectivism. In a word, here is all humanity circling with fatal monotony about the Providential fulcrum — the 'convoy wheeling encirculing abound the gigantig's lifetree'. Enough has been said, or at least enough has been suggested, to show how Vico is substantially present in the Work in Progress. Passing to the Vico of the Poetics we hope to establish an even more striking, if less direct, relationship.

Vico rejected the three popular interpretations of the poetic spirit, which considered poetry as either an ingenious popular expression of philosophical conceptions, or an amusing social diversion, or an exact science within the reach of everyone in possession of the recipe. Poetry, he says, was born of curiosity, daughter of ignorance. The first men had to create matter by the force of their imagination, and 'poet' means 'creator'. Poetry was the first operation of the human mind, and without it thought could not exist. Barbarians, incapable of analysis and abstraction, must use their fantasy to explain what their reason cannot comprehend. Before artic-

ulation comes song ; before abstract terms, metaphors. The
figurative character of the oldest poetry must be regarded, not
as sophisticated confectionery, but as evidence of a poverty-
stricken vocabulary and of a disability to achieve abstraction.
Poetry is essentially the antithesis of Metaphysics : Metaphysics purge the mind of the senses and cultivate the disem-
bodiment of the spiritual ; Poetry is all passion and feeling
and animates the inanimate ; Metaphysics are most perfect
when most concerned with universals ; Poetry, when
most concerned with particulars. Poets are the sense, philosophers the intelligence of humanity. Considering the Schol-
astics' axiom : '*niente è nell'intelleto che prima non sia nel
senso*', it follows that poetry is a prime condition of philosophy and civilization. The primitive animistic movement
was a manifestation of the '*forma poetica dello spirito*.'

His treatment of the origin of language proceeds along
similar lines. Here again he rejected the materialistic and
transcendental views : the one declaring that language was
nothing but a polite and conventional symbolism ; the other,
in desperation, describing it as a gift from the Gods. As
before, Vico is the rationalist, aware of the natural and inevitable growth of language. In its first dumb form, language
was gesture. If a man wanted to say 'sea', he pointed to the
sea. With the spread of animism this gesture was replaced
by the word : 'Neptune'. He directs our attention to the fact
that every need of life, natural, moral and economic, has its
verbal expression in one or other of the 30 000 Greek divini-
ties. This is Homer's 'language of the Gods'. Its evolution
through poetry to a highly civilized vehicle, rich in abstract
and technical terms, was as little fortuitous as the evolution
of society itself. Words have their progressions as well as
social phases. 'Forest-cabin-village-city-academy' is one rough

progression. Another : 'mountain-plain–riverbank'. And every word expands with psychological inevitability. Take the Latin word : 'Lex'.

1.	Lex	=	Crop of acorns.
2.	Ilex	=	Tree that produces acorns.
3.	Legere	=	To gather.
4.	Aquilex	=	He that gathers the waters.
5.	Lex	=	Gathering together of peoples, public assembly.
6.	Lex	=	Law.
7.	Legere	=	To gather together letters into a word, to read.

The root of any word whatsoever can be traced back to some pre-lingual symbol. This early inability to abstract the general from the particular produced the Type-names. It is the child's mind over again. The child extends the names of the first familiar objects to other strange objects in which he is conscious of some analogy. The first men, unable to conceive the abstract idea of 'poet' or 'hero', named every hero after the first hero, every poet after the first poet. Recognizing this custom of designating a number of individuals by the names of their prototypes, we can explain various classical and mythological mysteries. Hermes is the prototype of the Egyptian inventor : so for Romulus, the great law-giver, and Hercules, the Greek hero : so for Homer. Thus Vico asserts the spontaneity of language and denies the dualism of poetry and language. Similarly, poetry is the foundation of writing. When language consisted of gesture, the spoken and the written were identical. Hieroglyphics, or sacred language, as he calls it, were not the invention of philosophers for the mysterious expression of profound thought, but the common necessity of primitive peoples. Convenience only begins to assert itself at a far more advanced stage of civilization, in the form of alphabetism. Here Vico, implicitly at least, distinguishes between writing and direct expression. In such direct expression, form and content are inseparable. Examples are the medals of the Middle Ages, which bore no inscription and were a mute testimony to the feebleness of conventional alphabetic writing : and the flags of our own day. As with Poetry and Language, so with Myth. Myth, according to Vico, is neither an allegorical expression of general philosophical axioms (Conti, Bacon), nor a derivative from particular peoples, as for instance the Hebrews or Egyptians, nor yet the work of isolated poets, but an historical statement of fact, of actual contemporary phenomena, actual in the sense that they were created out of necessity by primitive minds, and firmly believed. Allegory implies a threefold intellectual operation : the construction of a message of general significance, the preparation of a fabulous form, and an exercise of considerable technical difficulty in uniting the two, an operation totally beyond the reach of the primitive mind. Moreover, if we consider the myth as being essentially allegorical, we are not obliged to accept the form in which it is cast as a statement of fact. But we know that the actual creators of these myths gave full credence to their face-value. Jove was no symbol : he was terribly real. It was precisely their superficial metaphorical character that made them intelligible to people incapable of receiving anything more abstract than the plain record of objectivity.

Such is a painful exposition of Vico's dynamic treatment of Language, Poetry and Myth. He may still appear as a mystic to some : if so, a mystic that rejects the transcendental in every shape and form as a factor in human development, and whose Providence is not divine enough to do without the cooperation of Humanity.

On turning to the ' *Work in Progress* ' we find that the mirror is not so convex. Here is direct expression — pages and pages of it. And if you don't understand it, Ladies and Gentlemen, it is because you are too decadent to receive it. You are not satisfied unless form is so strictly divorced from content that you can comprehend the one almost without bothering to read the other. This rapid skimming and absorption of the scant cream of sense is made possible by what I may call a continuous process of copious intellectual salivation. The form that is an arbitrary and independent phenomenon can fulfil no higher function than that of stimulus for a tertiary or quartary conditioned reflex of dribbling comprehension. When Miss Rebecca West clears her decks for a sorrowful deprecation of the Narcisstic element in Mr. Joyce by the purchase of 3 hats, one feels that she might very well wear her bib at all her intellectual banquets, or alternatively, assert a more noteworthy control over her salivary glands than is possible for Monsieur Pavlo's unfortunate dogs. The title of this book is a good example of a form carrying a strict inner determination. It should be proof against the usual volley of cerebral sniggers : and it may suggest to some a dozen incredulous Joshuas prowling aroud the Queen's Hall, springing their tuning-forks lightly against finger-nails that have not yet been refined out of existence. Mr. Joyce has a word to say to you on the subject : ' Yet to concentrate solely on the literal sense or even the psychological content of any document to the sore neglect of the enveloping facts themselves circumstantiating it is just as harmful ; etc.' And another : 'Who in his hearts doubts either that the facts of feminine clothiering are there all the time or that the feminine fiction, stranger than the facts, is there also at the same time, only a little to the rere ? Or that one may be separated from the orther ? Or that both may be contemplated simultaneously ? Or that each may be taken up in turn and considered apart from the other ?'

Here form *is* content, content *is* form. You complain that this stuff is not written in English. It is not written at all. It is not to be read — or rather it is not only to be read. It is to be looked at and listened to. His writing is not *about* something; *it is that something itself.* (A fact that has been grasped by an eminent English novelist and historian whose work is in complete opposition to Mr Joyce 's). When the sense is sleep, the words go to sleep. (See the end of '*Anna Livia*') When the sense is dancing, the words dance. Take the passage at the end of Shaun's pastoral : 'To stirr up love's young fizz I tilt with this bridle's cup champagne, dimming douce from her peepair of hideseeks tight squeezed on my snowybreasted and while my pearlies in their sparkling wisdom are nippling her bubblets I swear (and let you swear) by the bumper round of my poor old snaggletooth's solidbowel I ne'er will prove I'm untrue to (theare !) you liking so long as my hole looks. Down.' The language is drunk. The very words are tilted and effervescent. How can we qualify this general esthetic vigilance without which we cannot hope to snare the sense which is for ever rising to the surface of the form and becoming the form itself ? St. Augustine puts us on the track of a word with his '*intendere*'; Dante has : '*Donne ch'avete intelletto d'amore*', and ' *Voi che, intendendo, il terzo ciel movete* '; but his ' *intendere*' suggests a strictly intellectual operation. When an Italian says to-day ' *Ho inteso,* ' he means something between ' *Ho udito* ' and ' *Ho capito* ', a sensuous untidy art of intellection. Perhaps ' apprehension ' is the most satisfactory English word. Stephen says to Lynch : ' Temporal or spatial, the esthetic image is first luminously apprehended as selfbounded and selfcontained upon the immeasurable background of space or time which is not it....... You apprehend its wholeness.' There is one point to make clear : the Beauty of ' *Work in Progress* ' is not presented in space alone, since its adequate apprehension depends as much on its visibility as on its àudibility. There is a temporal as well as a spatial unity to be apprehended. Substitute ' and ' for ' or ' in the quotation, and it becomes obvious why it is as inadequate to speak fo ' reading ' ' *Work in Progress* ' as it would be extravagant to speak of ' apprehending ' the work of the late Mr. Nat Gould. Mr. Joyce has desophisticated language. And it is worth while remarking that no language is so sophisticated as English. It is abstracted to death. Take the word ' doubt ' : it gives us hardly any sensuous suggestion of hesitancy, of the necessity for choice, of static irresolution. Whereas the German ' Zweifel ' does, and, in lesser degree, the Italian ' dubitare '. Mr. Joyce recognises how inadequate ' doubt ' is to express a state of extreme uncertainty, and replaces it by ' in twosome twiminds '. Nor is he by any means the first to recognize the importance of treating words as something more than mere polite symbols. Shakespeare uses fat, greasy words to express corruption : ' Duller shouldst thou be than the fat weed that rots itself in death on Lethe wharf '. We hear the ooze squelching all through Dickens's description of the Thames in ' *Great Expectations* '. This writing that you find so obscure is a quintessential extraction of language and painting and gesture, with all the inevitable clarity of the old inarticulation. Here is the savage economy of hieroglyphics. Here words are not the polite contortions of 20th century printer's ink. They are alive. They elbow their way on to the page, and glow and blaze and fade and disappear. ' Brawn is my name and broad is my nature and I ' ve breit on my brow and all's right with every feature and I'll brune this bird or Brown Bess's bung ' s gone bandy '. This is Brawn blowing with a light gust through the trees or Brawn passing with the sunset. Because the wind in the trees means as little to you as the evening prospect from the Piazzale Michelangiolo — though you accept them both because your non-acceptance would be of no significance, this little adventure of Brawn means nothing to you — and you do not accept it, even though here also your non-acceptance is of no significance. H. C. Earwigger, too, is not content to be mentioned like a shilling-shocker villain, and then dropped until the exigencies of the narrative require that he be again referred to. He continues to suggest himself for a couple of pages, by means of repeated permutations on his ' normative letters ', as if to say : ' This is all about me, H. C. Earwigger : don't forget this is all about me ! ' This inner elemental vitality and corruption of expression imparts a furious restlessness to the form, which is admirably suited to the purgatorial aspect of the work. There is an endless verbal germination, maturation, putrefaction, the cyclic dynamism of the intermediate. This reduction of various expressive media to their primitive economic directness, and the fusion of these primal essences into an assimilated medium for the exteriorisation of·thought, is pure Vico, and Vico, applied to the problem of style. But Vico is reflected more explicitly than by a distillation of disparate poetic ingredients into a synthetical syrup. We notice that there is little or no attempt at subjectivism or abstraction, no attempt at metaphysical generalisation. We are presented with a statement of the particular. It is the old myth : the girl on the dirt track, the two washerwomen on thé banks of the river. And there is considerable animism : the mountain ' abhearing ', the river puffing her old doudheen. (See the beautiful passage beginning : ' First she let her hair fall and down it ftussed '.) We have Type-names : Isolde — any beautiful girl : Earwigger — Guinness's Brewery, the Wellington monument, the Phoenix Park, anything that occupies an extremely comfortable position between the two stools. Anna Livia herself, mother of Dublin, but no more the only mother than Zoroaster was the only oriental stargazer. ' Teems of times and happy returns. The same anew. Ordovico or viricordo. Anna was, Livia is, Plurabelle's to be. Northmen's thing made Southfolk's place, but howmultyplurators made eachone in person. " Basta ! Vico and Bruno are here, and more substantially than would appear from this swift survey of the question. For the benefit of those who enjoy a parenthetical sneer, we would draw attention to the fact that when Mr. Joyce's early pamphlet " *The Day of Rabblement* " appeared, the local philosophers were thrown into a state of some bewilderment by a reference in the first line to '' The Nolan. " They finally succeeded in identifying this mysterious individual with one of the obscurer ancient Irish kings. In the present work he appears frequently as '' Browne & Nolan " the name of a very remarkable Dublin Bookseller and Stationer.

To justify our title, we must move North, ' *Sovra'l bel fiume d'Arno alla gran villa* '... Between ' *colui per lo cui verso — il meonio cantor non è più solo* ' and the '' still to-day insufficiently malestimated notesnatcher, Shem the Penman ", there exists considerable circumstantial similarity. They both saw how worn out and threadbare was the conventional language of cunning literary artificers, both rejected an approximation to a universal language. If English is not yet so definitely a polite necessity as Latin was in the Middle Ages, at least one is justified in declaring that its position in relation to other European languages is to a great extent that of mediaeval Latin to the Italian dialects. Dante did not adopt the vulgar out of any kind of local jingoism nor out of any determination to assert the superiority of Tuscan to all its rivals as a form of spoken Italian. On reading his ' *De Vulgari Eloquentia* ' we are struck by his complete freedom from civic intolerance. He attacks the world's Portadownians : ' *Nam quicumque tam obscenae rationis est, ut locum suae nationis delitosissimm credat esse sub sole, huic etiam præ cunctis propriam volgare licetur, idest maternam locutionem. Nos autem, cui mundus est patria...* etc. ' When he comes to examine the dialects he finds Tuscan : ' *turpissimum...... fere omnes Tusci in suo turpiloquio obtusi....... non restat in dubio quin aliud sit vulgare quod quaerimus quam quod attingit populus Tuscanorum.* ' His conclusion is that the corruption common to all the dialects makes it impossible to select one rather than another as an adequate literary form, and that he who would write in the vulgar must assemble the purest elements from each dialect and construct a synthetic language that would at least possess more than a circumscribed local interest : which is precisely what he did. He did not write in Florentine any more than in Neapolitan. He wrote a vulgar that *could* have been spoken by an ideal Italian who had assimilated what was best in all the dialects of his country, but which in fact was certainly not spoken nor ever had been. Which disposes of the capital objection that might be made against this attractive parallel between Dante and Mr. Joyce in the question of language, i. e. that at least Dante wrote what was being spoken in the streets of his own town, whereas no creature in heaven or earth ever spoke the language of 'Work in Progress' It is reasonable to admit that an international phenomenon might be capable of speaking it, just as in 1300 none but an inter-regional phenomenon could have spoken the language of the Divine Comedy. We are inclined to forget that Dante's literary public was Latin, that the form of his Poem was to be judged by Latin eyes and ears, by a Latin Esthetic intolerant of innovation, and which could hardly fail to be irritated by the substitution of ' *Nel mezzo del cammin di nostra vita*' with its ' barbarous ' directness for the suave elegance of : ' *Ultima regna canam, fluido contermina mundo,* ' just as English eyes and ears prefer : ' Smoking his favourite pipe in the sacred presence of ladies ' to : ' Rauking his flavourite turfco in the smukking precincts of lydias. ' Boccaccio did not jeer at the ' *piedi sozzi* ' of the peacock that Signora Alighieri dreamed about.

I find two well made caps in the ' *Convivio*', one to fit the collective noodle of the monodialectical arcadians whose fury is precipitated by a failure to discover '' innocefree '' in the Concise Oxford Dictionary and who qualify as the ' ravings of a Bedlamite' the formal structure raised by Mr. Joyce after years of patient and inspired labour : ' *Questi sono da chiamare pecore e non uomini ; chè se una pecora si gittasse da una ripa di mille passi, tutte l'altre le andrebbono dietro ; e se una pecora per alcuna cagione al passare d'una strada salta, tutte le altre saltano, eziando nulla veggendo da saltare. E io ne vidi già molte in un pozzo saltare, per una che dentro vi salto, forse credendo di saltare un muro*'. And the other for Mr. Joyce, biologist in words : ' *Questo* (formal innovation) *sarà luce nuova, sole nuovo, il quale sorgerà ore l'usato tramonterà e darà luce a coloro che sono in tenebre e in oscurità per lo usato sole che a loro non luce.* ' And, lest he should pull it down over his eyes and laugh behind the peak, I translate ' *in tenebre e in oscurità* ' by ' bored to extinction. ' (Dante makes a curious mistake speaking of the origin of language, when he rejects the authority of Genesis that Eve was the first to speak, when she addressed the Serpent. His incredulity is amusing : ' *inconvenienter putatur tam egregium humani generis actum, vel prius quam a viro, foemina profluisse.* ' But before Eve was born, ' the animals were given names by Adam, the man who ' first said goo to a goose '. Moreover it is explicitly stated that the choice of names was left entirely to Adam, so that there is not the slightest Biblical authority for the conception of language as a direct gift of God, any more than there is any intellectual authority for conceiving that we are indebted for the ' Concert' to the individual who used to buy paint for Giorgione).

We know very little about the immediate reception accorded to Dante's mighty vindication of the ' vulgar ', but we can form our own opinions when, two centuries later, we find Castiglione splitting more than a few hairs concerning the respective advantages of Latin and Italian, and Poliziano writing the dullest of dull Latin Elegies to justify his existence as the author of ' *Orfeo* ' and the ' *Stanze* '. We may also compare, if we think it worth while, the storm of ecclesiastical abuse raised by Mr. Joyce's work, and the treatment that the Divine Comedy must certainly have received from the same source. His Contemporary Holiness might have swallowed the crucifixion of ' *lo sommo Giove* ', and all it stood for, but he could scarcely have looked with favour on the spectacle of three of his immediate predecessors plunged head-foremost in the fiery stone of Malebolge, nor yet the identification of the Papacy in the mystical procession of Terrestial Paradise with a ' *puttana sciolta* '. The ' *De Monar-*

chia ' was burnt publicly under Pope Giovanni XXII at the instigation of Cardinal Beltrando and the bones of its author would have suffered the same fate but for the interference of an influential man of letters, Pino della Tosa. Another point of comparison is the preoccupation with the significance of numbers. The death of Beatrice inspired nothing less than a highly complicated poem dealing with the importance of the number 3. in her life. Dante never ceased to be obsessed by this number. Thus the Poem is divided into three Cantiche, each composed of 33 Canti, and written in terza rima. Why, Mr. Joyce seems to say, should there be four legs to a table, and four to a horse, and four seasons and four Gospels and four Provinces in Ireland ? Why twelve Tables of the Law, and twelve Apostles and twelve months and twelve Napoleonic marshals and twelve men in Florence called Ottolenghi ? Why should the Armistice be celebrated at the eleventh hour of the eleventh day of the eleventh month ? He cannot tell you because he is not God Almighty, but in a thousand years he will tell you, and in the meantime must be content to know why horses have not five legs, nor three. He is conscious that things with a common numerical characteristic tend towards a very significant interrelationship. This preoccupation is freely translated in his present work : see the ' Question and Answer ' chapter, and the Four speaking through the child's brain. They are the four winds as much as the four Provinces, and the four Episcopal Sees as much as either.

A last word about the Purgatories. Dante's is conical and consequently implies culmination. Mr. Joyce's is spherical and excludes culmination. In the one there is an ascent from real vegetation — Ante-Purgatory, to ideal vegetation — Terrestial Paradise : in the other there is no ascent and no ideal vegetation. In the one, absolute progression and a guaranteed consummation : in the other, flux — progression or retrogression, and an apparent consummation. In the one movement is unidirectional, and a step forward represents a net advance : in the other movement is non-directional — or multi-directional, and a step forward is, by definition, a step back. Dante's Terrestial Paradise is the carriage entrance to a Paradise that is not terrestial : Mr. Joyce's Terrestial Paradise is the tradesmen's entrance on to the sea-shore. Sin is an impediment to movement up the cone, and a condition of movement round the sphere. In what sense, then, is Mr. Joyce's work purgatorial ? In the absolute absence of the Absolute. Hell is the static lifelessness of unrelieved viciousness. Paradise the static lifelessness of unrelieved immaculation. Purgatory a flood of movement and vitality released by the conjunction of these two elements. There is a continuous purgatorial process at work, in the sense that the vicious circle of humanity is being achieved, and this achievement depends on the recurrent predomination of one of two broad qualities. No resistance, no eruption, and it is only in Hell and Paradise that there are no eruptions, that there can be none, need be none. On this earth that is Purgatory, Vice and Virtue — which you may take to mean any pair of large contrary human factors — must in turn be purged down to spirits of rebelliousness. Then the dominant crust of the Vicious or Virtuous sets, resistance is provided, the explosion duly takes place and the machine proceeds. And no more than this ; neither prize nor penalty ; simply a series of stimulants to enable the kitten to catch its tail. And the partially purgatorial agent ? The partially purged.

THE IDEA OF TIME IN THE WORK
OF JAMES JOYCE

BY

MARCEL BRION

THE IDEA OF TIME
IN THE WORK OF JAMES JOYCE

BY

Marcel BRION.

Certain thinkers have at times wondered if the essential difference existing between man and God were not a difference of time. Space is not concerned here — God is everywhere — but, rather, this much more complex dimension which is generally inaccessible to human science. We measure time but we do not know what it is.

We often encounter in mystical literature the story of the monk or poet who has fallen asleep in the forest. When he awakes he no longer recognizes either men or the countryside. His meditation or slumber, which to him has appeared very short, has in reality lasted hundreds of years. But during this moment in which he has been snatched from the tyranny of time he has caught a glimpse of the mysterious aspects of infinity, he has neared the laws of the Cosmos, the throne of God.

Theoretically, the difference in speed between two objects in motion is sufficient to make them imperceptible to each other; to destroy, practically, their existence.

The relations between human beings are those of time.

All men are made similar by the nearly equal cadence of their heart-beats, but they are separated by the rhythms of their sensations or their thoughts. Only those walking at the same pace know each other.

The fourth dimension is actually the only one that matters. Space is nothing — it is reduced every day by mechanical means of communication — but consider two men seated side by side. They do not live in the same time. There is no possible communication between them. And it is often the tragedy of life to feel oneself only a few centimeters away from the beings among whom one lives, yet separated from them by all the infinity of time.

Time is not an abstract concept. On the contrary, it is perhaps the only reality in the world, the thing which is the most concrete. All the rest could only intervene in the form of its emanations.

We may deduce from this that time is the essential factor in a work of art. (This appears quite evident when considered in one if its aspects — rhythm). It is the law of architecture and of painting. The painters who have attained the greatest emotional power are precisely those whose work includes time — for example, Rembrandt. While we look at it, the picture seems always in the process of " being made ". It seems to be constructing itself with the moments and it seems that if we were to return on the morrow we should find it changed. And, in fact, when we return on the morrow, it is changed. There are likewise masterpieces of sculpture which give the impression of a continual palpitation, of an uninterrupted succession of imperceptible movements. It is this that is ordinarily called life — but life is the consciousness of time.

A book's story may embrace several decades, several centuries without revealing time to us. Another imposes it in a brief moment. There are flat books and deep books (without metaphor and almost in a material sense) ; there are also books rich with time and books destitute of time. This is the reason that one of the greatest writers of our period, one of the most sensitive and most intuitive, made of time the essential dimension of his work — *temps perdu* and *temps retrouvé*.

Marcel's Proust's idea of time is extremely curious. In his books time is a character like the others — I might even say more than the others. Time is at the centre of his work like a sort of lighthouse with turning signals. The men who revolve around this luminous mass are suddenly illuminated by the beams of the projector in periodic flashes, and the moment the light abandons them they fall back into obscurity, nothingness.

It is in time that the characters of Proust become conscious of themselves. They seek themselves in it and are reflected in it. They complete their metamorphosis in it. But time remains exterior to them. They are not incorporated in it any more than they integrate it in themselves. They submit to it, as to gravity or the law of acceleration. But the author has conceived it so intensely that we feel this time to be materialized often like an object, applied like a thin and transparent pellicle on the face of men.

Perhaps because illness sheltered him from the customary rhythm of life, because it imposed upon him a different order of sensations, Proust understood time as a thing in itself, time which does not ordinarily separate us from our act and which we make simply a condition, an accessory of our existence.

With James Joyce it is another thing. I place James Joyce and Marcel Proust together intentionally because in my opinion they are the two greatest writers of our century, the only ones who have brought an original vision of the world to our epoch, who have renewed equally the universe of sensations and of ideas. The work of Proust and that of Joyce are the only ones between which a parallel may be drawn on an ideal plane of quality — and this for reasons which go far beyond questions of technique or talent — in the domain of literature and art. Perhaps it is because a sort of pure instinct of genius is likewise found here under a very elaborate art ; but, above all, it is because with Joyce as with Proust time is a dominant factor.

On the absolute plane, the life of the ephemera and that of the animal endowed with the greatest length of life are equal. In the one case as in the other it is a life, and the fact that it stretches out for a few seconds or a few centuries has no importance. It is probable that both will be divided into a like number of units but that the unit will be long for the one and extremely short for the other. The idea of time being essentially that of the dissociation of moments, a hundredth of a second for an insect that lives for some minutes will be loaded with as many experiences as a year for the long-living animal. It it the same thing, all proportions retained, with men — some live at high speed, others at reduced speed ; and they are separated, inexorably most often, by these different cadences.

We may thus account for the fact that eighteen hours of Bloom's life should give birth to *Ulysses,* and we can easily imagine that *Ulysses* might have been ten times as long, a hundred times as long, extended to infinity, that one of Bloom's minutes might have filled a library. This is the mystery of the relativity of time.

If time remains external to Proust, if he gives it an existence apart, isolated from his characters, for Joyce, on the contrary, it remains the inseparable factor, the primary element at the base of his work.

This is why he creates his own time, as he creates his vocabulary and his characters. He soon elaborates what he receives from reality by a mysterious chemistry into new elements bearing the marks of this personality. But even as he metamorphoses the countryside, the streets of Dublin, the beach, the monuments, he mixes all this into what appears to us at first sight as a chaos. This chaos is the condition necessary to all creation. The cards are shuffled to begin a new game and all the elements of a universe are mingled before a new world is made, in order that new forms may be given birth. A total refutation of man and his milieu, a rejection of combinations already used, a need of fine new instruments. Joyce dashes the scenes of the world down pellmell to find an unhackneyed meaning and a law that is not outdated in the arrangement he is afterward to give them. To do this it is fitting that he should at the outset break through the too narrow restraints of time and space ; he must have an individual conception of these dimensions and adopt them to the necessities of his creation. In *Ulysses,* and still more in *Work in Progress,* we seem to be present at the birth of a world. In this apparent chaos we are conscious of a creative purpose, constructive and architectural, which has razed every conventional dimension, concept and vocabulary, and selected from their scattered material the elements of a new structure. Joyce has created his language, either by writing words phonetically — and Heaven knows such a method is enough to discipline English — or by introducing foreign words and dialect forms, or finally by the wholesale manufacture of words which he requires and which are not to be had at second hand. And it is all done with an unprecedented creative power, with an almost unique fertility of imagination, inexhaustibly reinforced by the incredible extent of his culture. In the field of verbal richness Joyce has annexed the seemingly impregnable position of Rabelais; but whereas in Rabelais, form was under no direction other than that of an amused fantasy, in Joyce it is the handmaid of a philosophy. *Work in Progress* seems to be based on the historical theory of Vico — an actual recreation of the world, its ideas and its forms.

Mr. Elliot Paul well demonstrated recently how Joyce in his composition of *Work in Progress* revealed an entirely individual conception of time and space.

This was already quite apparent in his first books. The stories in *Dubliners*, for example, seem entirely filled with the beating of a silent metronome. They unfold themselves in " time ". Properly speaking, *Araby* is a drama of time, a drama of lost time ; and we feel that each of the characters in *Dubliners* is rich or poor with his time, that the vibration of his life is hasty or slow.

In *Ulysses* the phenomenon is even more evident. To reduce the decades of the *Iliad,* the *Odyssey,* of Telemachus to eighteen hours in the life of a man — and of an ordinary man to whom nothing happens save the most ordinary events of existence — is one of the Einsteinian miracles of the relativity of time. And we understand it even better when we see the movement of the vibrations transformed in each chapter, changing rhythm and tempo, slowing up in the Nausicaa episode, blowing like the wind in that of Eolus, giving spacious and deep cadences to the gynecological discussion. The chapter most powerfully demonstrating Joyce's mastery in expressing time is perhaps that in which Marian Bloom's revery unrolls its rapid uninterrupted chain of ideas, memories and sensations, contrasting to her calm regular breathing.

Better than anyone else, Joyce has restored the sense of biological and intellectual rhythm. I imagine that he could write an unprecedented book composed of the simple interior physical existence, of a man, without anecdotes, without supernumeraries, with only the circulation of the blood and the lymph, the race of nervous excitations toward the centres, the twisting of emotion and thought through the cells. I imagine that Joyce could compose a book of pure time.

It sometimes seems that a page of Joyce is a strange vibration of cells, a swarming of the lowest Brownian movements under the lens of the microscope. In my opinion, if the recent books of Joyce are considered hermetic by the majority of readers it is because of the difficulty which the latter experience in falling into step, in adapting themselves to the rhythm of each page, in changing '' time '' abruptly and as often as this is necessary.

But still more than to *Ulysses* these remarks apply to the book which *transition* is publishing and of which we as yet know only a part. *Work in Progress* is essentially a time work. From a bird's eye view, time appears to be its principal subject. It begins in the middle of a moment and of a sentence, as if to place in infinity the initial disturbance of its waves. The concept of time here plays the principal role, not only by its concrete expressions but likewise by its abstract essence. It here takes on the significance of a creator-word and determines all the movements of the work.

The chronology of the story matters little to the author of *Work in Progress*. By his caprice, which in reality obeys a carefully studied and realized constructive will, characters most widely separated in time find themselves unexpectedly cast side by side ; and, as for example Mr. Elliot Paul recently wrote in *transition*, " Noah, Premier Gladstone and ' Papa ' Browning are telescoped into one ". This image is perfectly accurate, and the optics of the work are so much the less accessible to the average reader as he does not always distinguish the moment in which the present episode is placed. When we are made to pass, without any transition other than an extremely subtle association of ideas, from Original Sin to the Wellington Monument and when we are transported from the Garden of Eden to the Waterloo battlefield we have the impression of crossing a quantity of intermediary planes at full speed. Sometimes it even seems that the planes exist simultaneously in the same place and are multipled like so many '' over-impressions ". These planes, which are separated, become remote and are suddenly reunited and sometimes evoke a sort of accordeon where they are fitted exactly, one into another like the parts of a telescope, to return to Mr. Elliot Paul's metaphor.

This gift of ubiquity permits Joyce to unite persons and moments which appear to be the most widely separated. It gives a strange transparence to his scenes, since we perceive their principal element across four or five various evocations, all corresponding to the same idea but presenting varied faces in different lightings and movements.

It has often been said that a man going away from the earth at the speed of light would by this act relive in an extraordinarily short time all the events in the world's history. Supposing this speed were still greater and near to infinity — all these events would flash out simultaneously. This is what happens sometimes in Joyce. Without apparent transition, the Fall of the Angels is transparently drawn over the Battle of Waterloo. This appears to us as contrary neither to the laws of logic nor to those of nature, for these " bridges " are joined with a marvellous sense of the association of ideas. New associations, created by him with amazing refinement, they cooperate in creating this universe, the Joycian world, which obeys its own laws and appears to be liberated from the customary physical restraints.

And we have, indeed, the impression of a very individual world, very different from our own, a world of reflections that are sometimes deformed, as in concave or convex mirrors, and imprinted with a reality true and whole in itself. I do not speak here only of the vocabulary which Joyce employs and which he transforms for his usage — which, one might, say, he creates — but especially of his manners of treating time and space. It is for this reason, much more than because of the work's linguistic difficulties, that the reader often loses his footing. This is related to the prodigious quantity of intentions and suggestions which the author accumulates in each sentence. The sentence only takes on its genuine sense at the moment that one has discovered its explanatory *rapprochements* or has situated it in time.

And if the books of Joyce are as difficult for many to read as those of Einstein it is perhaps because both of these men have discovered a new aspect of the world and one which cannot be comprehended without a veritable initiation.

Translated from the French by ROBERT SAGE.

JAMES JOYCE'S *WORK IN PROGRESS* AND OLD NORSE POETRY

BY

FRANK BUDGEN

JAMES JOYCE'S *WORK IN PROGRESS* AND OLD NORSE POETRY

BY

Frank Budgen.

Joyce is not to be described by an etiquette or located within the four walls of any aesthetic creed. His logic is that of
life and his inventions are organic necessities. His present
work therefore, it seems to me, is best understood by what
has preceded it, his own in the first place and then its kin-
dred among past productions.

His mediaeval Catholic affinities have been often indicated
but while not denying the catholic-Irish element in Joyce —
its universality and its passionate localism — I think I can
see a kinship, equally authentic, with heathen Scandinavia.
The whole of Joyce's work has been hitherto one long cele-
bration of the principal city of the Ostmen. (If tomorrow
Dublin were spirited away it could be reconstructed out of
" Ulysses "). His genius is theirs — adventurous, secular,
and logical.

In the Edda we find the same sense of continuous creation
as in Joyce's *Work in Progress*. The world and the Gods
were doomed but phoenix like they were to rise again. The
Sun bore a daughter before the Wolf swallowed her. Vidor
and Vali found on the grass the golden tables of the stricken

gods and Thor's hammer fell into the mighty hands of his two sons. Joyce writes : " The oaks of ald now they lie in peat yet elms leap where ashes lay. Phall if you but will, rise you must : and none so soon either shall the pharce for the nunce come to a set down secular phoenish. "

Joyce is at present reconquering and extending a poetic freedom partly usurped by the working intelligence. Human speech has always had two functions. It seems expedient that a number of men building a tower shall attach fixed meanings and logical relationships to the words they use but when not actually working, the words become as free as their users and are as able and willing to lay aside their union cards doff their overalls and dance. In *Work in Progress* they are dancing new figures to a new tune. The Norse poet also was alive to the immense emotional force of indirect and allusive speech as a principle of leverage applied to the imagination. He called a Spade a Spade and a Ship a Ship when he was using the one or the other. But as a poet he loaded his song with Kennings so that the image of the thing besung might appear with new life out of the multicoloured mosaic of its attributes and associations.

The language and thought of Europe have since been enriched with ten centuries of cultural effort. Technical progress has brought the sundered tribes of Europe nearer together. Their interests interlock and their thought and speech interpenetrate in spite of wars and customs barriers. Joyce's material is therefore infinitely richer and more varied. He has at his disposal all the legends not only of his own tribe but of all the human race, and he is surrounded by a social organisation immeasurably vaster and more complex than that of viking Scandinavia. All languages and dialects are there for him to draw on at will and the shop talk of all trades and the slang of all towns. Like every great craftsman he freely makes use of all that he finds existing and adds thereto his own inventions. In this connections it seems curious that the inventor of a wireless gadget or of a patent medicine may burden the dictionary with a new compound but that the poet shall be forbiddden an expressive word because it has never been used before. For Joyce's purpose no word is unpoetic — none obsolete. Words fallen out of use are racial experience alive but unremembered. When in the poet's imagination the past experience is relived the dormant word awakes to new life and the poet's listeners are lifted out of their social, functional grooves and partake of the integral life of the race. The average literary snob would reject half the material that Joyce uses and no one but an artist of sovereign freedom and tireless logic could subdue such headstrong stuff to the purpose of his design.

Necessarily, for every one poetic device of the skald Joyce must have a hundred. The kenning was extensive. In every case the theme was expanded. Odin was the Wielder of Gungni; Thor, Hrungni's bane, God of Goats, Hallower of Earth; Sleep, a parliament of dreams; the eye, a cauldron of tears; a ship, a plank bear, and so on. The object was imaginatively reborn in the light of each new name. The universality of Joyce's theme dictates an intensive technique — a greater density of word texture. Meanings can no longer lie side by side. Here they overlap and there into one word he crowds a whole family of them. A letter added or left out — the sound of a vowel or consonant modified — and a host of associations is admitted within the gates. And one letter may stand pregnant with meaning as a rune. Through this singular compactness a page of Joyce's composition acquires some of the potency of a picture. The words seem to glitter with significance as they lie on the printed page. We speak them and they flow like a river over our consciousness evoking images vivid and unexpected as those of a dream.

The Eddic poet tells us Odin had two ravens, Thought and Memory. He sent them out into the world every day (" and he loosed two croakers from under his tilt, the groud Phenician rover "). Thought he loved, but if Memory came not back, how could he endure the loss? This expresses the normal human valuation. Next to the wish to live lies the wish to remember — after experiencing we want to possess ourselves of our experiences through memory. Modern art and modern psychology witness how strong is this urge in the individual. He recaptures for himself and hears from the lips of others the story of his earliest days. He pursues his dreams to the places where they hide, finds them and adopts them. He hates his drunken brother but pastes pictures of his grotesque antics in the family album. In *Work in Progress* the poet's imagination seems one with racial memory. Human society in its groups, tribes, nations, races, searches the earth and its legends for the story of its beginning. But it is not as an historical hypothesis that Joyce recreates for us the birth of the city (" Twillby, Twillby "). The growth of the spoken and written word (" if you are abcedminded ") — the invention of tools, born of " Moppa Necessity mother of Injins ". It is rather as if these things were personal experiences once forgotten and by a prodigious effort of memory brought to mind.

I see a large humanity in Joyce's work. None of his contemporaries is so free from highbrow snobbishness and the superiority complex. The characters in Ulysses are of the common run of average humanity. Joyce didn't find them at hunt balls, country house parties and the Chelsea Studios of millionaire dilettanti but in trams, pubs, shops and the common streets and houses where the mass of the people spend their lives. *Ulysses* is one day in a certain town but the Adventures of the living and thinking body are as understandable everywhere and at any time as music or a drawing.

And the persons in *Work in Progress* are as universal as the words through which they live. Adam and Eva, Cain and Abel, Michael and Lucifer, the god who walked in the Garden of Eden and his contemporaries who thundered from the skies of Greece and Scandinavia, the wandering brother of the wide open spaces and the brother of intellectual experiences — antagonistic and inseparable. They are the representative persons of the mind of the human race. The difficulty in entering into the imaginative world of Work in Progress lies in no unessential obscurity on Joyce's part but in our own atrophied word sense due in large measure to the fact that our sensibilities have been steam-rollered flat by a vast bulk of machine made fiction. The reader is becoming rarer than the writer. The words of dead poets are read and confirmed like the minutes of the previous meeting, with perhaps the dissentient voice of one Scotch shareholder. Taken as read? Agreed. Agreed. (Sonnet 43, When most I wink ") But " *Work in Progress* " is obviously the next business on the agenda paper, and if the words of a contemporary are not as plain as a soap advertisement on a hoarding there is an outcry as if no mystery in poetry had ever been. Every poet's work has always presupposed the necessary religious and mythical knowledge on the part of his hearers and an active imagination to follow identity through change.

The Jute and Mutt dialogue (Transition No. 1) besides being a passage of great beauty and a good example of Joyce's

recreation of our poetic tongue, is essentially northern in character. If stick and stone had speech to tell the story of more
transient shapes this is surely their authentic utterance and
this their unmistakeable character, humorous, harmless and
earthy. Only in the Edda where wise giant and Sybil and
wiser god discuss the origin and destiny of the world do I find
a similar sense of the mystery of creation, Mutt and Jute
approach each other like the vast slow moving figures on stilts
out of some dreamt-of pantomine and their greetings are the
purposeful and significant misunderstandings of slapstick
comedians.

Jute : Are you Jeff ?

Mutt : Some hards.

Jute : But you are not jeffmute ?

Mutt : Noho.   Only an utterer.

Jute : Whoa ?   Whoat is the mutter with you ?

They mimic the tribute giving and taking of vanished generations as clowns holding the stage after the exit of great an-
tagonists.

Jute : Let me cross your qualm with trink gilt.   Here have
sylvan coyne, a piece of oak.

Mutt : Louee, louee ! How wooden I not know it, the
intellible greyt-cloak of Cedric Silkyshag !... Here where the
liveries, monomark.   There where the missers mooney Min-
nikin passe.

The echo of the clamour of a great battle appears to them
ghostlike.

Mutt : Just how a puddinstone inat the brook cells by a
river pool.

Jute : Load Allmarshy !   Wid wad for a Norse like ?

Mutt : Somular with a bull on a clompturf.   Rooks roa-
rum rex roome !   I could snore to him of the spumy horn,

with his woolseley side in, by the neck I am sutton on, did Brian d' of Linn.

Shapes of land and water moulded by elemental forces, compel, in their turn, the placing of cities and habitations of mankind. Mutt calls Jute to witness : —

" Walk a dun blink round this allbutisle and you skull see how olde ye plaine of my Elters, hunfree and ours, where wone to wail whimbrel to peewee o'er the saltings, where wilby citie by law of isthmon, where by a droit of signory, icefloe was from his Inn the Byggning to whose Finishthere Punct. "

And further he sees a thousand years of human destinies crowded into the silence and fury of a snowstorm on a river : —

" Countlessness of live stories have nether fallen by this plage, flick as flowflakes, litters from aloft, like a waast wizzard all of whirlworlds. Now are all tombed to the mound, isges to isges, erde from erde. Pride, O pride, thy prize ! "

Settler and raider lie buried together and out of their dust arise new forms of life : —

Mutt : Meldundleize ! And thanacestross mound have swollup them all. This ourth of years is not save brickdust and being humus the same roturns. He who runes may rede it on all fours.

And as the unwilling Sybil sinks to the underworld and the old giant forfeits his wagered head and the god departs, so the familiar spirits of this river valley become again silent and immobile.

Mutt : Ore you astonaged, jute you ?

Jute : Oye am thonthorstrok, thing mud.

The Scandinavian poet treated his gods familiarly as being human like himself. Joyce does the same ; and singularly enough the similarity extends to their special treatment of the thunder god. Loki flouts each brother and sister deity in turn. He derides the cowardice of the brave, confounds the virtuous with their vices and jeers at the peacemaker for his fruitless meddling. The entry of the thunder god silences him. " For I know that thou wilt strike ". In Ulysses the thunder god, disguised as phenomenon, interrupts a discussion on birth control with similar effect. His role in " *Work in Progress* " is still more important. Here he is ever present, woven as a coloured strand in a tapestry, side by side with all other elemental human values. Fear of a soaking, fear, at most, of a lightning struck chimney pot or doubt as to the efficiency of lightning conductors is all that most of us are capable of experiencing at the approach of a thunderstorm. But we may be sure that Thor was a living god before he got pensioned off as a myth. We hear him in *Work in Progress*, as in the Edda, the friend and affrighter of man, present at the origins of human society as the inspirer of that fear which is the beginning of wisdom.

The many names and states of Mr. Earwicker recall those of Odin with his legion of names — Grimni at Geirrod's, Valfather on the battlefield, Ygg on the scaffold, Bolverk on the harvest field, Gangleri going up and down the world observing and learning Out of his own labour and a woman's sufferings he got the gift of song. He learned how to get off with women and how to get on with them, how to drink ale with friends, when to speak and when to be silent and he passed on his knowledge to his juniors. In his multiple personality and his sum of human experience Mr. Earwicker is of Odin's kin. But Odin feels mental and physical pain. He loses an eye and he hangs nine nights on a wind-swept tree, offered, a sacrifice, himself to himself. In Joyce's intensely bright composition all human experience is transposed into a key of glittering humour which is the essential province of the intelligence. He discovers in and extracts out of every phase of human experience its intelligent counterpart as a painter distils out of his motive its essence of colour.

Work in Progress gives a bird's eye view of the time landscape. We see it all at once — as in a section of Earth laid bare by a landslide we see the changes of a million years lying exposed in a few square feet.

I walked with Mr. Bloom, pro tem. traveller in Space-time over Essex Bridge, Sat with him eating liver and bacon in the Ormond hotel, heard with him the Clock Strike nine, stood guard over Stephen and went home with him. In *Work in Progress* it is I alone who am compelled ideally to move from the Garden of Eden to Eden Quay in the turn of a word those Elements which are the personages of Joyce's book being appropriately present anywhere at any time.

Thus the beginning of the world and the events of today may lie side by side embedded in the rhythm of last year's catch phrase ("Ere beam slewed cable or Derzherr, live wire, fired Benjermine Funkling outa th' Empyre, Sin righthand Son"). Ancient fable and new fact — starting point and goal become one. Dramatic conflict in its sexual, racial, social manifestations is presented as implicit in its characteristic sign, —

construct ann aquilittoral dry ankle...

Whatever the elements brought together they have the rightness of a dream wherein all things we ever knew or experienced occur not in their time sequence but according to their necessary importance in the pattern dictated by the dream's own purpose and logic. And this I take to be the key to the understanding of *Work in Progress* and the secret of its peculiar beauty. In Ulysses is the life — real life — of day ; here the reality — super reality — of night. The liver and bacon that Bloom ate was limited — not alluring perhaps, but smellable, tasteable and filling, whereas the vast appetite of Shaun is fed on mountains of provoking but unsubstantial food. " While the loaves are aflowering and the nachtingale jugs. " And there is abundant refreshment for the mourners at Finnegan's wake but they are warned. — " But, lo, as you would quaffoff his fraudstuff and sink teeth through that pyth of a flowerwhite bodey, behold of him as behemoth for he is nowhemoe ", Joyce has penetrated into the night mind of man, his timeless existence in sleep, his incommunicable experiences in dreams. He is under the spell neither of sleep nor dream but in this vast unexplored province he has found the material with which he is writing the life and adventures of the human mind.

PROLEGOMENA TO WORK IN PROGRESS

BY

STUART GILBERT

PROLEGOMENA TO *WORK IN PROGRESS*

BY

Stuart GILBERT.

" Great poets are obscure for two opposite reasons ; now, because they are talking about something too large for anyone to understand and now, again, because they are talking about something too small for anyone to see. " With this preamble Chesterton introduces his study of that profoundest of nineteenth-century English poets, Francis Thompson. " In one of his poems ", Chesterton continues, " he says that the abyss between the known and the unknown is bridged by ' pontifical death '. There are about ten historical and theological puns [1] in that one word. That a priest means a pontiff, that a pontiff [2] means a bridge-maker, that death certainly

---

1. *Quoi de plus divertissant et de plus instructif, tout ensemble, qu'un beau calembour étymologique?* (Victor Bérard : *l'Odyssée*, p. 106) The importance of Homeric influences on James Joyce's work can hardly be overestimated, and it is noteworthy that the Odyssey begins with a pun on the name of its hero :

οὔ νύ τ' 'Οδυσσεὺς
'Αργείων παρὰ νηυσὶ χαρίζετο ἱερὰ ῥέζων
Τροίῃ ἐν εὐρείῃ ; τί νύ οἱ τόσον ὠδύσαο, Ζεῦ ;

Odyssey I. 60-62.

2. With this use of " pontiff " a passage from the Anna Livia (Anna Liffey) section of Mr Joyce's work, which, in some respects, reminds one of a

is a bridge, that death may turn out to be a reconciling priest, that at least priest and bridges both attest to the fact that one thing can get separated from another thing — these ideas, and twenty more, are all tacitly concentrated in the word ' pontifical ' ". It is not an accident that in casting about for some anticipation in English literature of the uncompromising brilliance of James Joyce's latest work (for, after all, poets are born not made, and — unless another miracle be presumed — the conception of a poet cannot be wholly immaculate), the first name that suggests itself should be that of Francis Thompson, that Crashaw '' born again, but born greater ''. For Thompson, too, wrote of '' something too large for anyone to understand ", and since infinite greatness is — but for certain flashes when our sight is focussed to a god's-eye view of the universe — intellectually and linguistically out of our reach, not only is the poet's vision, in itself, difficult of apprehension, but the language of common speech must often prove inadequate to express concepts perceived *sub specie æternitatis*.

There are, in fact, two difficulties (or, rather, two aspects of the same difficulty) to disconcert a reader of *Work in Progress*. Perplexed, he poses first the essential question '' What is it all about ? '' adding, *sotto voce*, a plaintive afterthought '' Why, anyhow, does the author make it so difficult ? [1] ''

Homeric '' catalogue '' — in this case, of rivers, their names welded into words — may be compared. '' Do you know she was calling backwater girls from all around to go in till him, her erring man, and tickle the pontiff aisy-oisy ? ''

[1]. It is significant that these questions *What is it all about?* and *Why does the author make it so difficult?* are the very *cris de cœur* of Everyman when some unforeseen catastrophe makes of him a target for the arrows of outrageous fortune, and, baffled by this seemingly wanton cruelty, he asks himself what on earth or in heaven the Demiurge was about when He contrived his laby-

The subject of *Work in Progress* may easiest be grasped by a reference to Vico's *Scienza nuova,* a treatise on the philosophy of history which appeared about two hundred years ago. The reception of Vico's work was that which too often awaits the philosopher attempting a new synthesis of the disparate phenomena which make up world-history. The story goes that a contemporary *savant*, Capasso, after an unsuccessful attempt to digest Vico's work, ran ostentatiously to his doctor to have his pulse taken, and a certain Neapolitan noble, asked for news of the writer, tersely replied " Off his head ! " Vico proposed the making of " an ideal and timeless history in which all the actual histories of all nations should be embodied ". Human societies begin, he contended, develop and have their end according to certain fixed laws of rotation ; there is a recurrent cycle in human " progress ", as in the astronomical domain. (Observe the subtle implications of the title *Work in Progress*). But this natural history of man is not, as might be expected, to be discovered by a mere series of inductions from past events. The essential facts are embodied in the lives, true or legendary, of national heroes; they are revealed through human personalities, rather than by acts or events. In his preface to Vico's works Michelet has succinctly set out this relation between the heroic personality and the so-called " facts " of history. " The principle of the *New Science* is this : humanity is its own creation. The heroes of myth, Hercules whose arms rend the mountains, Lycurgus or Romulus, law-givers who in a man's lifetime accomplished the long work of cen-

rinthine universe. Thus, too, Mr. H. G. Wells' young giant, seeing for the first time the crowded confusion of modern life (vide *The Food of the Gods*), mutters : " I don't understand... What are all you people doing with yourselves ? What's it all for ? What is it all for and where do I come in ? "

turies — all these are creations of the peoples' thoughts. God alone is great. When man craved for men-like-gods he had his way by combining generations in an individual, by incarnating in a single hero the ideas of a whole cycle of creation. Thus he fashioned his historical idols, a Romulus or a Numa. Before these shadowy heroes the peoples made obeisance. But the philosopher bids them rise : ' That which you adore', he says, ' is but yourselves, your own conception '. Hitherto mankind believed that all progress was due to chance appearances of individual genius. Political, religious, poetic advance was ascribed to the unexplained talent of certain individuals, splendid but incomprehensible. History was a sterile show, at best a diverting shadow-play. " The aim of the new science was to illustrate the fundamental unity of history, God's work in progress, which is not based (as, at first sight, it would seem) on sporadic advances due to the accidental genius of individuals, but on a general and inevitable movement of mankind as a whole, a trend recurrent and predictable like that of the tides, embodied, crystallized in great personalities. Thus, speaking of the ' sages', Vico remarks that " Solon was neither more nor less than the people of Athens, awakened to consciousness of its rights, the true founder of democracy. Dracon was simply the emblem of an aristocratic tyranny which preceded the change. " " The diversity of views as to Homer's birthplace forces us to the conclusion that, when the various races of Greece disputed among themselves the honour of claiming him as one of theirs, it was because *they themselves were Homer.* "

Vico places the beginnings of human history one or two centuries after the Deluge. The earth had grown dry and a storm brooded dark above the hills, on whose summits lonely giants roamed. Suddenly sounded a crash of thunder and,

" terrified by this happening whose reason they ignored, they raised their eyes and gazed for the first time heavenwards". That was the beginning of what we call civilisation. Their fear of the sky (the heavens personify the first of the gods to all primitive peoples) was the beginning of wisdom. It drove them to refuge in dark caverns of the earth and thus arose the idea of the family and man's first attempt at 'virtue'. Hitherto, these giants, like beasts of the field, had fornicated openly with the female of the moment. Now, after the sky-god had spoken by his thunder, they were ashamed of open coition ; each took to his cave a single woman and with her, in darkness, founded a family. Thus, for Vico, the etymology of 'Jupiter' is *jus + pater* : the sky is not merely the allfather but also the source of law and justice, of the family tie and social consciousness. But not only did the voice of the thunder inspire the brutish giants with ideas of shame and justice ; the strong emotion of their fear loosened their tongues and they ejaculated the first monosyllable of the language, the name of father, that word which in all tongues has the same root. It is significant that *Work in Progress* opens with a crash of thunder.

James Joyce's new work, in fact, (as far as can be judged from the portion of it which *Transition* has so far published) is, in one of its aspects, a realization of the Italian philosopher's conception of an " ideal history "; those " eternal laws which all nations observe in their beginnings and developments, in their decay and death, laws which, if world upon world were born in infinite eternity, would still hold good for those new worlds ". Under the variety of external forms there is an essential identity between all peoples, all histories, which is embodied in the legends and lives of their national heroes. *Work in Progress* is, indeed, a book of heroes, many of whom are merged in the panheroic figure of H. C. E. (Here Comes Everybody). Vico's work, moreover, is much preoccupied with the root-meanings of words (their associative rather than strictly etymological implications) and he " contemplated the formation of a ' mental vocabulary ' ", whose object would be to explain all languages that exist by an ideal synthesis of their varied expressions. And now, after two centuries, such a synthesis of history and of language, a task which seemed almost beyond human achievement, is being realised by James Joyce in his latest work.

To a certain extent, therefore, the verbal difficulties ot *Work in Progress* are accounted for by the nature of the subject. It is obvious that in this composite picture of the life of mankind, where mythical heroes of the past, characters of biblical legend and notabilities of recent times are treated as one and the same protagonist, the style was bound to reflect the kaleidoscopic permutations of the temporal, physical and spatial attributes of the " hero ". But in the verbal structure of Mr Joyce's new work there is a personal element which had already manifested itself in *Ulysses* and was, strangely enough, overlooked even by appreciative critics. Thus, in a recent study of *Ulysses* a commentator quotes at length the following passage from the opening of the *Oxen of the Sun* (Lying-in Hospital) episode and condemns it as "unconditionally inept and unpardonable ". " Merely to arrange words in the form of a Chinese puzzle is pointless. It is unfortunate that Mr Joyce has chosen to commit this folly so many times in a work of such significance. " The passage is as follows.

" Universally that person's acumen is esteemed very little perceptive concerning whatsoever matters are being held as most profitably by mortals with sapience endowed to be studied who is ignorant of that which the most in doctrine erudite and certainly by reason of that in them high mind's ornament deserving of veneration constantly maintain when by general consent they affirm that other circumstances being equal by no exterior splendour is the prosperity of a nation more efficaciously asserted than by the measure of how far forward may have progressed the tribute of its solicitude for that proliferant continuance which of evils the original if it be absent when fortunately present constitutes the certain sign of omnipollent nature's incorrupted benefaction. "

The obscurity of that passage, its prolixity and redundancy — all are deliberate, and artistically logical. For this whole episode of the *Oxen of the Sun* is constructed so as to follow the growth of the embryo from its dark and formless origin to the hour of its emergence into the light of day, a fully developed and perfected child. The style of this section of *Ulysses* is at first dark and shapeless. Gradually the diction takes form and clarifies itself till it culminates in a futurist cacophony of syncopated slang, the jargon of our latest and loudest *jeunesse nickelée*. But, before this outburst, the language ascends in orderly march the gamut of English styles — of Mallory, Mandeville, Bunyan, Addison, Sterne, Landor, Macaulay, Ruskin, Carlyle and others. (It may be noted, however, that, as in the unborn embryo there is often premature development of a certain part, so there are occasional patches in the first section of the *Oxen of the Sun* where the terseness and clarity of later styles are anticipated.)

In the *Sirens* episode, again, the structure of the chapter strictly follows the form of a *fuga per canonem*. Not only this, but the terminology is chosen so as to include musical metaphors and terms. '' Fall flat '', '' sound as a bell '',

" all for his own gut ", " stave it off " — these and many other such idioms were deliberately selected for their musical associations.

The literary device employed by Mr Joyce in these episodes is not, as might appear at first sight, a mere caprice or *tour de force*, but has its justification in the origins of human speech. The earliest language was (as Vico points out) that of signs ; the human animal was, in fact, dumb. He indicated the subject of his thought by pointing a finger at the object. The next stage was the naming of objects by ejaculated monosyllables. Then the name of the thing itself was used by extension to signify a wider, even an abstract, concept. From this view of the origin of language it follows that the use of simile and trope was not, as is generally believed, a poetic artifice, but was imposed on primitive man by the very conditions of his development and limits of his vocabulary. If we talk of the mouth of a river, for instance, we do not use the word ' mouth ' because it seems a felicitous metaphor but because the makers of the language could conceive of no possible alternative ; indeed, unless we have recourse to scientific jargon, no better term has yet been invented. In carefully adapting his words to his subject-matter, Mr Joyce is not performing a mere conjuring-trick with the immense vocabulary he has at his command but is going back to the original and natural methods of human speech. By extension, in such passages as that quoted above, the adaptation of words to subject was carried into the domain of style ; but the principle remained the same — the fixing of the reader's mind on the subject-matter by every possible means, the exploitation of every potentiality of the language to create a complete harmony between form and content.

A common error on the part of both professional and amateur critics is that of applying to new literary forms the quasi-ethical test : `` Would I wish *all* modern literature to be composed after this model ? '' That test of the universal (of doubtful value even in the domain of conduct) is quite inapplicable to original works of art. It is, rather, the criterion of a masterpiece of literature that it stands alone, and this holds good as well for diction as for form and content. The unusual word-formation of *Work in Progress,* a constructive metabolism of the primal matter of language, was called for by its subject and is thereby justified, but it will in all probability remain a unique creation — once and only once and by one only. For it is inconceivable that such a method of writing could prevail in general or narrative literature and it would be wrong to see in *Work in Progress* the promise of a systematic disintegration of language, or any sort of propaganda for an international tongue, a new Volapük or Esperanto. Indeed, disciples of the New Word would defeat their own ends. The word-building of *Work in Progress* is founded on the rock of petrified language, of sounds with solid associations ; were this groundwork to be undermined by a general decomposition of words, the edifice would in time be submerged in the shifting sand of incoherence, there would be a dissolution of logical speech and thought and in the last end man would revert to his brutish state, as it was in the beginning before the Lawfather thundered.

A dangerous game, in truth, the *jeu de mots,* this vivisection of the Word made Flesh ! But so, perhaps, was creation itself — the rash invention of a progressive Olympian with a penchant for practical jokes.

A consciousness of this `` joky '' side of creation pervades *Work in Progress.* The world is indeed a Wonderland of perpetual surprises for every Alice of us. In the *reductıo ad absurdum* of the processes of human thought — for absurdity is latent there behind the looking-glass of logic — Lewis Carroll, that elfin dialectician, excelled; it is noteworthy that he, too, experimented in the composition of picturesque and amusing neologisms, "portmanteau words" as his Humpty Dumpty called them. But Carroll's inventions were exclusively English and went no further than the telescoping of English words together, whereas the Irish writer's vocabulary is world-wide — *Work in Progress* may well be easier reading for a polyglot foreigner than for an Englishman with but his mother tongue — and he compresses allusions rather than single words. The difference can best be shown by quotation. Here are two familiar lines from Carroll's "Jabberwocky".

> 'Twas brillig, and the slithy toves
> Did gyre and gimble in the wabe.

They are explained as follows.

"That's enough to begin with", Humpty Dumpty interrupted: "there are plenty of hard words there. '*Brillig*' means four o' clock in the afternoon — the time when you begin *broiling* things for dinner... '*Slithy*' means 'lithe and slimy'. You see it's like a portmanteau — there are two meanings packed up into one word... '*Toves*' are something like badgers — they're something like lizards — and they're something like corkscrews... To '*gyre*' is to go round and round like a gyroscope. To '*gimble*' is to make holes like a gimlet."

Humpty Dumpty might have added that "*brillig*" also suggests the sunshiny hours and "*gimble*" implies "gambol"; but no doubt he guessed that Alice, a clever little girl, could see these allusions for herself.

With these a few lines from *Work in Progress* may now be compared. "**Not all the green gold that the Indus contains would over hinduce them (o. p.)** [1] **to steeplechange back to their ancient flash and crash habits of old Pales time** [2] **ere beam slewed cable or Derzherr, live wire, fired Benjermine Funkling outa th'Empyre, sin right hand son...** "

The last words of this passage are built on an old music-hall refrain, popular in those ' good old days ' when the " Empire " in Leicester Square was the happy-hunting-ground of the pretty ladies of London town : " There's hair, like wire [3], coming out of the Empire. " An electrical undercurrent traverses the whole of this passage, which alludes to the dawn of pre-history when Vico's thunderclap came to rescue man from his wild estate ; the "**flash and crash days** ". "**Beam slewed cable** " hints at the legend of Cain and Abel, which is frequently referred to in *Work in Progress*. "There's hair" has crystallized into "**Derzherr**" — *Der Erzherr* (arch-lord) — with a sidethrust at the hairy God of illustrated bibles. He is a "**live wire** "— a bustling director. "Benjamin " means literally " son-of-the-right-hand " ; here the allusion is to Lucifer (the favourite archangel till his rebellion) as well as to Benjamin Franklin, inventor of the lightning-conductor. The end of his name is written " — **jermine** ", in tune with

1. " our people " : indicated by the preceding passage.
2. Pales, the oldest of woodland gods: " Palestine " is also implied.
3. " Hair like wire ", curiously enough, brings us back to Lewis Carroll. who may have had some part in the procreation of the phrase. Isa Bowman in her *Story of Lewis Carroll* (p. 24), speaking of his insistence on accuracy, relates : " I remember how annoyed he was when, after a morning's sea bathing at Eastbourne, I exclaimed : ' Oh this salt water, it always makes my hair as stiff as a poker ! ' He impressed it on me quite irritably that no little girl's hair could ever possibly get as stiff as a poker. ' If you had said *stiff as wires,* it would have been more like it ' " Cf. Shakespeare, Sonnet 130.

the German word *Erzherr*, which precedes, and " **Funkling** "
(a diminutive of the German *Funke* — a spark), which follows.
Also we can see in this word a clear, if colloquial, allusion to
the angel's panic flight before the fires of God. In the back
ground of the passage a reference to the doom of Prometheus,
the fire-bringer, is certainly latent. " **Outa** " — the America-
nism recalls "**live wire** ", as well as such associations as
" outer darkness " — Lucifer's exile in the void. "**Empyre** "
suggests *Empyrean*, highest heaven, the sphere of fire (from
" *pyr* ", the Latinized form of the Greek root " *pur* " — fire)·
Finally, **sin** implies at once the German possessive *sein* (his),
and the archangel's fall from grace.

This passage illustrates the manner in which a *motif* foliates
outwards through the surrounding text, beginning from a single
word — here the " flash " in " **flash and crash** " has " elec-
trified " the words which follow, and a German formation
has similarly ramified into the context. All through *Work
in Progress* similar foliations may be traced, outspreading,
overlapping, enmeshed together ; at last deciduous, as new
and stronger *motifs* thrust upwards into the light. The difference in texture between such complexity and Carroll's occasional use of " portmanteau words " is evident. A similar contrast can be established between the neologies of
Work in Progress and the new-coined words of Edward
Lear, which, though they have not the same currency as Carroll's, are no less rich in verbal humour. Lear, too, had a
gift for depicting droll or fantastic personages.

His Waistcoat and Trowsers were made of Pork Chops ;
His Buttons were Jujubes and Chocolate Drops ;
His Coat was all Pancakes with Jam for a border.
And a girdle of Biscuits to keep it in order ;

And he wore over all, as a screen from bad weather,
A Cloak of green Cabbage-leaves stitched all together.

In this " nonsense rhyme " of Lear, *The New Vestments,*
there is a curious anticipation of the idea of comestible dress
developed by Mr Joyce in a description of Shaun's apparel
(*Transition*, n° 12) ; his " **star-spangled zephyr... with his motto
through dear life embrothered over it in peas, rice and yeggyolk,** "
and his " **gigot turnups** "

Lear's method of dovetailing words together (" scroobious ",
" slobaciously ") may be compared to an Englishman's way
of carving a leg of mutton ; he cuts vertically through the
meat of sound and the fat of common sense, with an eye only
to the funny effect of the chunk removed ; whereas the Irish
writer (like Tristan at the *découpage* of the deer and to the
wonderment of Mark's knights) carves his *gigot* in the conti-
nental manner, that is to say, parallel to the etymological
bone, following the way the muscles are naturally and anato-
mically set. Again, like Gibbon's " solemn sneer ", Lear's
humour often depends on pairs of words, usually adjectives,
unequally yoked together. " *All the bluebottle flies began to
buzz at once in a sumptuous and sonorous manner, the melodious and mucilaginous sounds echoing all over the waters and
resounding across the tumultuous tops of the transitory Tit-
mice upon the intervening and verdant mountains with a serene
and sickly suavity.* " A travesty of Gibbon's use of paired
words is found in *Ulysses*. " Silent in unanimous exhaustion and approbation the delegates, chafing under the length
and solemnity of their vigil and hoping that the joyful occur-
rence would palliate a licence which the simultaneous absence
of abigail and officer rendered the easier broke out at once
into a strife of tongues. " In *Work in Progress* the treatment

of pairs of ideas is *symbolical*, in the exact meaning of that word; ideas are *fused together*. Thus in " **gigot turnups** " we have the ideas of leg-of-mutton sleeves and their inferior counterpart, pegtop trousers, turned up in the modern manner, fused into one. Both Lear and Joyce exploit the incongruous, basis of all humour, but, while Lear's incongruities are laid side by side in comic pairs, Joyce's are *symbolised*, merged in one — the exact opposite of the Lear-Gibbon hendiadys. This fusion of ideas is illustrated in the description of the tree of life, " **our sovereign beingstalk,** " and the " **origin of spices** " (*Transition*, n° 15). Lear's *extravaganze* are airy nothings, soaring on dual wings of candid nonsense, whereas Mr Joyce's for all their subtle buoyancy, are gravid with the seeds of red magic.

There is also a radical contrast between the humour of Carroll and Lear and the almost demoniac ribaldry of parts of *Work in Progress*. In the lines quoted above it is significant that the nearly meaningless catch of a London music-hall song should serve Joyce as the warp whereon to weave the story of divine reprisal on a revolting archangel. Of all the aspects of *Work in Progress* this, perhaps, will prove the most disconcerting to the general reader. The boisterous joviality of certain passages, the verbal horseplay, for instance, of that pastmaster of conceit, Jaunty Jaun, will certainly offend those who hold that gravity should exclude buoyancy in treating of first and last things. But, after all, the terms " heavy " and " light " are relative ; birth and death, the story of the Fall, God's mysterious ways to man — all these are tragic or absurd according to the observer's standpoint ; exclusive seriousness, indeed, is a colour-blindness of the intellect.

Given the subject of *Work in Progress*, the form and language employed followed as a matter of course. The personality of H. C. E., polymorphous yet strangely self-consistent, heroic yet human all-too-human, dominates the book from its broken beginning, the point arbitrarily chosen (since for time-bound man a beginning there must be) for us to set foot upon the circular track of the New History. The difficulties of the text are conditioned by the subject, for the language is world-wide as the theme. Words are built up out of sounds whose associations range over many frontiers, whose echoes ricochet from the ends of the earth. In this spectral realm of gigantic shadows, of river and mountain seen nearly or dimly as the nightclouds now lift now close in again, lies revealed the ageless panorama of the race, our own world and yet another. To comprehend this new vision of a timeless world something is needed of the clairvoyant audacity of Francis Thompson's last poem :

> O World invisible, we view thee,
> O World intangible, we touch thee,
> O World unknowable, we know thee,
> Inapprehensible, we clutch thee !

II

The foregoing remarks may, it is hoped, suffice to give a general view of the method and scope of *Work in Progress*, but it may not be unprofitable to add a pratical illustration of the manner in which to read the work (perhaps not without some mental effort, certainly with ultimate enjoyment) and look for the allusions embedded, obscurely sometimes, it cannot be denied, and beneath the surface, in the text. The following passage is taken from the fragment published in

Transition No. 13 (pp. 17-19) and is reprinted with permission of the editor and author.

Sis dearest, Jaun added, with voise somewhit murky as he turned his dorse to her to pay court to it, melancholic this time whiles his onsaturncast eyes in stellar attraction followed swift to an imaginary swellaw, O, the vanity of Vanissy! All ends vanishing! Pursonally, Grog help me, I am in no violent hurry. If time enough lost the ducks walking easy found them. I'll nose a blue fonx with any tristys blinking upon this earthlight of all them that pass by the way of the deerdrive or wilfrid's walk but I'd turn back as lief as not if I could only spoonfind the nippy girl of my heart's appointment Mona Vera Toutou Ipostila, my lady of Lyons, to guide me by gastronomy under her safe conduct. That's more in my line. I'd ask no kinder of fates than to stay where I am, under the invocation of Saint Jamas Hanway, servant of Gamp, lapidated, and Jacobus A Pershawm, intercissous, for my thurifex, with Peter Roche that frind of my boozum, leaning on my cubits, at this passing moment by localoption in the birds' lodging me pheasants among, with me hares standing up well and me longears dittoes till well on into the beausome of the exhaling night, picking stopandgo jewels out of the hedges and catching dimtop brilliants on the tip of my wagger for them breezes zipping round by Drumsally do be devils to play fleurt. I could sit on safe side till the bark of Saint Grousers for hoopoe's hours, laughing lazy at the sheep's lightning, hearing the mails across the nightrives (peepet! peepet!) and whippoor willy in the woody (moor park! moor park!) as peacefed as a philopotamus, and crekking jugs at the grenoulls, leaving tea for the trout and belleeks for the wary, till I'd followed through my upfielded neviewscope the rugaby moon cumuliously godrolling himself westasleep amuckst the cloudscrums for to watch how carefully my nocturnal goosemother would lay her new golden sheegg for me down under in the shy orient. What wouldn't I poach — the rent in my riverside my otther shoes, my beavery, honest! — for a dace feast of grannom with the finny ones, flashing down the swansway, leaps ahead of the swift mac Eels and the pursewinded carpers, rearin antis rood perches astench of me, or, when I'd like own company best, with the help of a norange and bear, to be reclined by the lasher on my logansome, my g. b. d. in my f. a. c. e., solfanelly in my shellyholders and lov'd latakia the benuvolent, for my nosethrills with the jealosomines wilting away to their heart's deelight and the king of saptimber letting down his humely odours for my consternation, dapping my griffen, burning water in the spearlight, or catching trophies of the king's royal college of sturgeons by the armful for to bake pike and pie while, O twined me abower in L'Alouette's Tower, all Adelaide's naughtingerls, juckjucking benighth me, I'd tonic my twittynice Dorian blackbudds off my singasongapiccolo to pipe musicall airs on numberous fairyaciodes. I give, a king, to me, she does alone up there, yes see, I double give till the spinney all eclosed asong with them. Isn't that lovely though? I give to me alone I trouble give! And what sensitive coin I'd be possessed of, at Latouche's begor I'd sink it sumtotal, every dolly farting, in vestments of subdominal poteen at prime cost and I bait you the whole ounce you half on your backboard that I'm the gogetter that'd make it pay like cash registers. And, what with one man's fish and a dozen mens poissons, I'd come out with my magic fluke in close time, fair, free and frolicky, zooming tophole on the mart as a factor. And I tell you the Bectives wouldn't hold me. By the unsleeping Solman Annadromus, ye god of little pescies, nothing would stop me for mony makes multimony like the brogues and the kishes. Not the Ulster Rifles and the Cork Milice and the Dublin fusees and Connacht Rangers ensembled. I'd axe the chan-

non and leip a liffey and drink anny black water that rann onme
way. Yip! How's thats for scats, mine shatz, for a love-
bird ? To funk is only peternatural its daring feers divine.
Bebold! Like Varian's sweeping all behind me. Aud before you
knew where you weren't I stake my ignitial's davy, cash-and-
cash can-again, I'd be staggering humanity and loyally rolling you
over, my sponse, in my tous of red clover, fiehigh and fiehigher
and fiehighest of all. I'd spoil you altogether. Not a spot of my
hide but you'd love to seek and scanagain. There'd be no standing me, I tell you. And as gameboy as my pagan name K. C. is
what it is I'd never say let fly till I'd plant you, my Gizzygay, on
the electric ottoman in the lap of lechery simpringly stitchles
with admiracion among the most uxuriously furnished compart-
ments with sybarate cham bers just as I'd run my shoestring into
near a million of them as a firstclass dealer and everything. Only
for one thing that I'd be awful anxious, you understand, about
shoepisser pluvious and in assideration of the terrible luftsucks
playing around in the coold amstophere till the borting that
would perish the Dane and his chapter of accidents to be atramental to the better half of my alltoolyrical health, not considering my capsflap, an that's the truth now out of the cackling bag
for truly sure for another thing I never could tell the leest false-
hood that would truthfully give sotisfiction I'm not talking apple
sauce eithou. Or up in my hat. I earnst. Schue!

The above passage occurs in a sermon delivered by Jaunty
Jaun to his congregation of the twenty-nine girls who figure
as a " female plebiscite " in *Work in Progress*. The form
is that of a " lenten pastoral " and it is interesting to compare
Jaun's homily with the series of sermons delivered at the
" retreat " described in *A Portrait of the Artist as a Young
Man*. Jaun is the jovial, blustering type of Irishman who

believes in enjoying life, and the advice he gives to his chapel of girls is a cheerful counterblast to the comminations of the Jesuit priests. He has much to say about himself; he is a boaster, but, like many boasters, a bit of a coward. An expert in love-making, he is, one feels, an equally competent love-breaker. The mood of this excerpt is high-spirited fantasy; in texture it is lighter, and in allusion less esoteric, than those portions of the work which deal directly with the main theme; for these reasons, and because it suffers less by excision, this passage has been selected as a suitable introduction to the perusal of *Work in Progress*.

In the notes which follow explanation is given of nearly all the synthetic words or phrases. The commentary, however, does not claim to be exhaustive; some allusions have certainly been overlooked, a few (e. g. *Jacobus A. Pershawm, Varian's*) have remained insoluble; moreover, certain interpretations are merely tentative. Indeed, one of the fascinations of reading *Work in Progress* is that as a mine of suggestion and allusion it is practically inexhaustable; apart from its literary and cosmological innovations, the resolution of its synthetic word-structures may well have a special appeal to the present generation of the English-speaking races, whose interest in words — *parvis componere magna* — is demonstrated by the space reserved in contemporary journals for problems in word-building and word-manipulation.

Voise. — His voice, grown rather hoarse, suggests " noise ",
Somewhit. — A trifle less than " somewhat ".
Dorse. — He turns his *back* on her to pay court to his voice.
Onsaturncast. — *Upwards* (towards the planet) *plus* " uncertain " (timidly).

Stellar. — The allusion is to Dean Swift's Stella[1]; in the following sentence **Vanissy** (Vanessa) continues the motif.

Swellaw. — He swallows down an impediment in his throat, looking towards a bird that is not there, a projection of the " bird " allusion in " **swift** ". **Swellaw**, thus spelt, may also suggest celestial ordinance.

Pursonally. — He has been complaining that he wants more money ; Jaun is the sort of man who never has enough of it.

If time... them. — A variant of the proverb *Chi va piano va sano*. If Mr. Time-Enough lost his ducks, Mr. Walking-Easy found them.

I'll nose... fonx. — **Fonx** suggests " funk " (a blue funk) as well as " fox ".

With any tristys. — As well as any sad person (Tristram) alive on the earth.

Of all them... — An echo of the lines " O all you who pass by etc. "

Wilfrid's walk. — This appears to be a child's name for some animal (c. f. Teddy-bear).

1. As in *Ulysses*, so in *Work in Progress*, there are many references to " the awful Dean of St Patrick's ", and in a recent review of a fragment of Mr Joyce's latest work, published under the title *Anna Livia Plurabelle*, it was implied that the language of this work was akin to the " little language " in which Swift addressed MD. As the reviewer wittily observed, " a little language is a dangerous thing ". The comparison was, however, inapt. The prose of *Work in Progress* is far removed from a " little language " of lovers, or those pretty, petty diminutives coined by Presto for Pepette. It is, on the contrary, a *great* language, an augmentation of the resources of the common tongue, like a language of giants or Homer's " speech of the blessed gods ". Moreover, a little language is a sort of private code, significant only to those " in the know ". The peculiarity of Mr Joyce's latest work is its " catholicism ", and most of the difficulties of the text are due to the ubiquity of its allusions.

Spoonfind. — The ideas of " kiss " and " waitress " are combined, preparing for " **Lady of Lyons** " — the title of Bulwer Lytton's famous play and an allusion to a popular restaurant.

Mona Vera... — The one true Catholic (**toutou** i. e. fondling and everywhere) and Apostolic Church. Jaun would like to find a girl with a job of her own to support him so that he would not have to work. A teashop assistant would do — or (for Jaun is here in orders) the Church.

Saint Jamas Hanway. — Jonas Hanway (1712-1786) was the first man to walk the London streets carrying an umbrella. The Londoners threw stones at him.

Pershawm, intercissous. — I am unable to trace the history of this other holy martyr, who was " cut up ", as Hanway was stoned.

Thurifex. — Suggests *thurifer* and *crucifix*. Jaun is fond of his pipe ; further references to this come later. Tobacco is, in fact, his favourite incense.

Peter Roche. — " Thou art Peter, and upon this rock etc. " **Roche** also suggests *fish,* the roach as well as (I suppose) the *anguille sous roche*. From this point a " fish " motif begins to insinuate itself. Or, to vary the metaphor, this word sounds the tonic of the key for the following passage.

Frind of my boozum. — C. f. . a line from Moore's " *Meeting of the Waters* ". " 'Twas that friends, the beloved of my bosom, were near. "

Cubits. — *Elbows* plus *Cupids*.

With me hares... — He sees himself spending a night in the woods (Phoenix Park ?) amongst the animals. He will be rather frightened, his hair will stand on end, his ears pricked up (**longears** also implies " rabbits "). This part of

Jaun's sermon is a " pastoral " in both senses, and its language is redolent of the fauna of field and forest.

Beausome. — Suggests *bosom* and *beauty*.

Stopandgo jewels. — Glowworms.

Dimtop brilliants. — He will catch misty dew on the tip of his tongue.

Fleurt. — Recalls the French origin of the word " flirt " — *fleurette*.

Saint Grousers... — This seems to refer to the opening of the shooting season. Jaun will stay on the safe side till the lawful season for shooting begins ; " **hoopoes' hours** "(?).

Sheep's lightning. — Sheet lightning is to fork lightning as the sheep to the wolf.

Nightrives. — He hears the night mail-trains going along the river *banks*.

Moor park! — The cry of this Australian bird is said to be " More Pork " ! (c. f. **Adelaide's naughtingerls** below.) Also an allusion to Moor Park where Swift met Stella.

Philopotamus. — An apt variant of *hippopotamus*.

Crekking jugs... — He will crack jokes with the (Frenchy) frogs and his *genoux* will knock together with panic. **Crekking** recalls " brek-kek-koax " the classical " frogs' chorus ".

Leaving... trout. — Jaun is lazy; he will be too slack to bring home his picnic outfit. **Belleek** is a kind of china.

Neviewscope. — Cloud-gazing telescope; *nepheloscope*. (Allusion to Nevsky Prospect? Also, perhaps, to *nepotism ;* Jaun is sure to have an *amicus in curia*.)

Rugaby moon.... — *Rugby* plus *lullaby*. Jaun sees the moon rolling between the clouds like a ball between the muddy feet of the scrum. **Westasleep** suggests the song " *The West's asleep* " (lullaby motif). The moon " goes to sleep " when she reaches the limit of her course.

For to watch... — He will await sunrise.

The rent... — There is a hole in his trousers on the side towards the river. **Beavery** suggests *hat-beaver-breviary*.

Dace... grannom. — " Fishing " allusions. The *grannom* is a fly used by fishermen. The **feast of grannom** is probably some fishermen's festival.

Swansway. — A " *kenning* " for *river*.

Pursewinded. — Suggests *pursy* plus *short-winded*.

Rearin antis. — An echo of " *rari nantes* ". Jaun, of course, is an easy victor in the Liffey swimming match.

Astench. — *Astern* plus *tench* plus *stench*. They would get scent of Jaun, from behind, to leeward.

Norange. — The derivation of *orange* is *naranj* (Arab :). This is, in fact, the old form of the word (c. f. apron from *napperon*). There is here a hint of the *rainbow* motif which appears so often in the work.

Bear. — Besides the obvious meaning, the word *pear* (German *Birne*) is suggested, and the suffix " *or two* " (an orange or two) as in " carriage and pair ".

Logansome. — *Lonesome* plus *logan-stone* (a poised heavy stone at the river's edge).

G. b. d. in my f. a. c. e. — An ingenious combination of suggestions for both pipe-smokers and musicians (the notes on the " lines " G B D are between the " spaces " F A C E). The GBD pipe is well known.... Here a " music motif" begins to foliate.

Solfanelly. — Suggests the " tonic solfa " and *solfanelli* (Italian : matches).

Shellyholders. — Hands cupped like shells.

Benuvolent. — Italian forms continue. Full of clouds (*nuvoli*).

Jealosomines. — Jessamines *plus* jealous-of-mine.

2

Deelight. — The word " delight " is thus stressed in the duet " The Moon hath raised her lamp above ".

Saptimber. — Surely it is more reasonable thus to call the month than " the seventh ", when it is really our ninth !

Dapping. — A method of fishing. **Griffeen (?)**

Burning water. — The water would be lit up.

Pike and pie. — Suggests " by and by ". The *p* to *b* mutation was prepared for above.

O twined... — Echo of a song.

Adelaide's naughtingerls. — **Adelaide** recalls the song as well as the town.

I'd tonic... — I'd teach my nine-and-twenty blackbirds how to sing. (Echo of the nursery rhyme — with musical and floral variations.)

Numberous. — *Numerosus* (musical).

Fairyaciodes. — Variations (fairy — odes).

I give... — This is a translation of the " tonic solfa " names of the notes in the scale (as an Italian ear might hear them : *do,* " I give ", *re,* " a king ", and so on) : *do, re, mi, fa, sol, la, si, do.* **I double give** : the high *do* (C).

Eclosed. — *Echoed* plus (French) *éclore.*

I give to me... — This is the major chord (do-mi-sol-do : CEGC).

Sensitive. — Allusion to the *sensitive* (note preceding the tonic).

Latouche's. — Probably a business in which Jaun thinks of investing : the name is evidently chosen for its musical association (*les touches* — the keys of a piano). There is here a foliation of French words. The Latouche in question is, perhaps, one of the numerous Huguenot families settled in Dublin (c. f. Bloom's reflexions on Miss Dubedat : *Ulysses,* p. 167. **L'Alouette,** " a lark in clear air ", is also mentioned in *Ulysses ;* p. 8).

Subdominal. — Abdominal attuned to subdominant. Note how Jaun in (in) **vestments** combines, as usual, the lucrative with the ritual.

Bait. — *Bet* adapted to the " fish " motif.

Half... — " Sis " is lightly clad ; her garments of weigh but half an ounce.

Factor. — Besides the vague " business " allusion in this word there is a suggestion of the French *facteur*. One of Jaun's avatars is " **Shaun the Post** ".

Bectives. — A football team.

Solman Annadromous. — **Solman** [1] suggests (*inter alia*) " salmon " (a fish said to be sleepless). *Anadromous* — of fish ascending rivers to spawn. The ' n ' is doubled here so as to form " **Anna** ", a river prefix often used in *Work in Progress*. " Anna " seems to be a popular corruption of the Latin *amnis*; thus the Anna Liffey was shown in old maps as *Amnis Livius*. Anna Livia (the Eve of the story), " **a judyquean not up to your elb** ", holds, earlier in the work, a levée of some hundred of her namesakes from all parts of the earth, including Anna Sequana (Seine), Annie Hudson, Susquehanna and good Ann Trent.

Pescies. — Little fishes (Italian) with, perhaps, a suggestion of " sins " — *péchés*.

Brogues and kishes. — From the Irish expression " ignorant as a kish of brogues (a basketful of little shoes) ". Here the " loaves and fishes " are hinted at.

---

1. This association of Solomon and Salmon may be assimilated with the Irish legend of the " salmon of wisdom " ; to eat the smallest morsel of its flesh was (as in the the case of the national hero Finn MacCool) to acquire the gift of wisdon and prophesy (c. f. the " tree of knowledge " and Prometheus legends, strands of which are often discernable in the texture of *Work in Progress*).

Axe the channon. — **Channon** — " Shannon " *plus* " channel ".

Leip a liffey. — Nothing could hold up the advances of Jaun the lover. The **leip** formation may suggest the " salmon's leap " (Leixlip).

Annyblack water. — **Anny**, as above, for *amnis*. Three Irish rivers are called " Blackwater ".

Scats. — Norwegian for *treasure* ; in German *Schatz*.

Peternatural. — Peter, the " loganstone " of the Church, made a very human slip on three famous occasions.

Its daring... — This passage is obscure ; the obvious meaning is " It is divine to risk doing the thing one fears " ; but in this passage Jaun is making love and, from what precedes, seems to be indulging in a certain exhibitionism. The " forbidden fruit " idea, an invitation to some act out of the normal, seems to be implied.

And before... — This passage goes to the lilt of an Irish song. Jaun is swinging the girl higher and higher in his arms.

Ignitial's davy. — Jaun has a postman's lamp with him : also *affidavit* is implied.

Hide. — A recall of the " treasure " theme, as well as Jaun's skin.

Admiracion. — She simpers her admiration.

Sybarate..... — Separate *plus* sybarite. The separation has bisected **chambers.**

Run my shoestring. — (American) make easy money. The American note is appropriate, for Jaun is the sort of Irishman who crosses the ocean and makes his pile in the States.

Assideration... — Jaun thinks how cold it is out in the night under the stars (**assideration**). **Luftsucks,** a variant of the German *Luftzug*, a draught.

Borting. — His cold is getting worse and thus he snuffles " morning"; the Danish prefix for *departure* is *bort-*.

Perish the Dane. — Weather to perish the Danes — very cold weather. Here **Dane** suggests " Dean " (pronounced in the Irish manner) ; a recall of the " Swift " motif. The word " **chapter** " naturally ensues.

Atramental. — Detrimental *plus* " dark " (c. f. *atrabilious*).

Sotisfiction. — Satisfaction *plus* " so 'tis fiction ".

Eithou. — I — thou : either.

I earnst... — A sneeze is coming — **Schue** ! — Germanically antithetic to " **my hat** ", and he foreshortens his mendacious " I am in earnest ".

THE REVOLUTION OF LANGUAGE
AND JAMES JOYCE

BY

EUGENE JOLAS

THE REVOLUTION OF LANGUAGE
AND JAMES JOYCE

BY

Eugene Jolas.

The real metaphysical problem today is the word. The
epoch when the writer photographed the life about him with
the mechanics of words redolent of the daguerreotype, is
happily drawing to its close. The new artist of the word has
recognized the autonomy of language and, aware of the
twentieth century current towards universality, attempts to
hammer out a verbal vision that destroys time and space.

When the beginnings of this new age are seen in perspective,
it will be found that the disintegration of words, and their
subsequent reconstruction on other planes, constitute some of
the most important acts of our epoch. For in considering
the vast panorama of the written word today, one is struck
with the sensation of its endless and monotonous repetit-
iousness. Words in modern literature are still being set side
by side in the same banal and journalistic fashion as in preceding decades, and the inadequacy of worn-out verbal patterns
for our more sensitized nervous systems seems to have
struck only a small minority. The discovery of the subconscious by medical pioneers as a new field for magical explorations and comprehensions should have made it apparent that

the instrument of language in its archaic condition could no longer be used. Modern life with its changed mythos and transmuted concepts of beauty makes it imperative that words be given new compositions and relationships.

James Joyce, in his new work published serially in *transition*, has given a body blow to the traditionalists. As he subverts the orthodox meaning of words, the upholders of the norm are seized by panic, and all those who regard the English language as a static thing, sacrosanct in its position, and dogmatically defended by a crumbling hierarchy of philologists and pedagogues, are afraid. Epithets such as " the book is a nightmare, " "disgusting, distorted rubbish, " " a red-nosed comedian, " " senile decay of the intellect, " " utterly bad, " etc., have been poured on the author and his work.

In a recent essay in the *Criterion* entitled " Style and the Limitations of Speech, " Mr. Sean O'Faolain attempts to dispose of the Joycian onslaught by examining the nature of language and its limitations, and he arrives at the remarkable stand-pat conclusion of the " immobility of English. " Mr. O'Faolain states among other things : " There are real limitations to the eloquence of words. These are mainly two, despite the overteeming richness of what we do possess, our vocabulary is not of our manufacture and it is limited : and meanwhile, liberty to invent, and add to, and replace, is absolutely denied us — denied us, as it would seem, for all time. " Mr. O'Faolain, basing his conclusions on a dessicated philosophy of historicism, rejects Mr. Joyce's language as " a-historic, " and chides him for running counter to certain eternal laws of nature.

Again, in a review of *Anna Livia Plurabelle* (Irish Statesman, Dublin) after examining a phrase beginning with :

" She was just a young thin pale soft shy slim slip of a thing etc., " and after indicating that Mr. Joyce's system had collapsed, because he (the reader) was unable to penetrate the meaning of certain neologisms, Mr. O'Faolain concludes that this language is " almost music " and serves no useful pur) pose. The sentence he quotes, (from page 21 of A. L. P.- contains the word " silvamoonlake " which he analyses. This mental exercise ends in the recognition of silva as being in relation to silver and sylva, moon as being moon, and lake as being lake. That is already something, although lake should also be understood to have some relation to a lacteal, or milky, image (cf. P. 24 A. L. P. the Petrarca Laura allusion, " By that Vale Vowclose's lucydlac, etc. "). He stumbles against the neologism " forstfellfoss. " This means nothing to him. Now the word " foss, " which puzzles him more than " forst " and " fell, " — although the real meaning of " forst " has also escaped him, it being indicative of tree — is rather well known to students of geography. It is a geographical and topographical term which my Baedeker readily reveals to me. Under the heading of World's Biggest Waterfalls, I discover, not only Niagara Falls (170 m high) but Feigumfoss in Norway (656 m. high). I also find other falls in Norway bearing the generic ending of foss : Esplansfoss, Grandefoss, Hoenefoss, Stalheimsfoss, and many others. It has been a custom for some time to admit to English citizenship such geographical and topographical terms as : pampa, (ice) berg, spa, fjord, campagne, steppe, veldt, lock, savannah, geyser, maelstrom, lande, canyon, etc. Mr. O'Faolain will probably object that he is not supposed to know Scandinavian in order to understand a work of English literature. But it is equally apt to say that a knowledge of Latin and Greek, and a light smattering of other languages, is no longer sufficient in an age that is rapidly coming to a complete internationalization of the spirit.

Let it be understood once and for all that we can no longer accept the ideas of a past epoch. We are not interested in romantic " *passé-ism,* " nor in infantile parallelisms.

The most cursory glance at the evolution of English, or other languages, shows that speech is not static. It is in a constant state of becoming. Whether the organic evolution of speech is due to external conditions the people themselves bring about, or whether it is due to the forward-straining vision of a single mind, will always remain a moot question. I imagine there is an element of both working simultaneously at this process. Renan once accused Saint-Paul of " audaciously violating, if not the genius of the Greek language, at least the logic of human language. " The reason for Saint-Paul's heresy lies in the fact, — as pointed out by the Rev. Marcel Jousse — that he tried to follow the laws of spoken human language. There is no logical reason why the transmutation of language in our day should not be as legitimate as it was throughout the ages. While painting, for instance, has proceeded to rid itself of the descriptive, has done away with the classical perspective, has tried more and more to attain the purity of abstract idealism, and thus led us to a world of wondrous new spaces, should the art of the word remain static ? Is it not true that words have undergone rad_ ical changes throughout the centuries ? Should James Joyce, whose love of words and whose mastery of them has been demonstrated in huge creations, be denied the right (which the people themselves hold) to create a vocabulary which is not only a deformation, but an amalgamation of all the languages in the so-called English-speaking world ? The English language, after all, has been an amalgamation from

the very beginning of its existence. Why should the unilingual Englishman feel worried , when in the British Isles
alone, there are five languages still in common use: Manx,
English, Irish, Gaelic and Welsh ! With what right can the
"unilingual" Englishman demand that the well of the English
language remain undefiled ? It is a very muddy well, at
best.

But, says Mr. O'Faolain " a word is a fragment of history
that we have agreed to accept as a symbol for a limited number
of its own experiences and ours, and the writer works with
these experiences and our knowledge of them ; as a result,
words become in his hands most pliable, roguish and suggestive things. " To illustrate his point he chooses the word
" gentleman. " This example seems to me inept. If he
wishes to show that words do not change, then "gentleman"
does not show it. But to show that they do change, let us
take " title, " for example. The Latin word is " titulus "
which is the cross on top of the letter " t. " INRI was a
" titulus " for the cross of Christ. There is even a feastday
of that name in the Roman Catholic Church. To the lawyer
a " title " represents the authenticity of a document representing an heir's succession. When an American society girl
marries a duke or a marquis, she is marrying a " title. ".
Then " title " also indicates the descriptive term for a work
of literature. For Gene Tunney, the word " title " represents
the honor he received, after Mr. Jack Dempsey had seen the
starry firmament. Etc., etc.

While Mr. Joyce, beginning with *Ulysses*, and now in his
still unnamed work, has been occupied in exploding the
antique logic of words, analogous experiments have been
made in other countries. In France, Germany and Italy, the
undermining process has been going on for the past fifteen

years. In order to give language a more modern elasticity, to give words a more compressed meaning through disassociation from their accusomed connections, and to liberate the imagination with primitivistic conceptions of verbs and nouns, a few scattered poets deliberately undertook to disintegrate their own speech.

Léon-Paul Fargue, one of the great French poets of our age, has created astonishing neologisms in his prose poems. Although retaining much of the purity of French, he has slashed syllables, transposed them from one word to another, built new words from root vocables and thus introduced an element entirely unknown before into French literature. The large place he leaves to the dream as a means for verbal decomposition adds piquancy to his work. When, in *Tumulte*, he says: " Enclochez-vous dans l'alvéole ", no dictionary will give you the meaning of *enclocher*. Nor is the English translation, " enbell yourselves, " anything but a neologism. He says : " Te voilà, zoizonin, " which might be translated by " lilbirdie, " but which is a pure invention of his own. Consider also the phrase : " Anatole, tanaos et thanatos, anthropofrime, " etc. Or: " un vieux bec de gaz couronné, noir paponcle, " which was translated in *transition* by: " an old crowned gas lamp, black papuncle. "

The revolution of the surrealists, who destroyed completely the old relationships between words and thought, remains of immense significance. A different association of words on planes of the spirit makes it possible for these poets to create a universe of beauty the existence of which was never suspected before. Michel Leiris in his experimental *Glossaires* departs radically from academic ideas and presents us with a vocabulary of iconoclastic proportions. M. Leiris stated at one time : " A monstruous aberration makes men believe that language is born to facilitate their mutual relations. With usefulness as an aim, they prepare dictionaries, in which words are catalogued and given a well-defined meaning (so they think) based on custom and etymology. Now, etymology is a perfectly vain science that gives no information whatsoever about the veritable meaning of a word, i.e. the particular significance, the personal significance which everybody must give it, according to the pleasure of his spirit. As for custom, it is unnecessary to say that it is the lowest criterion one might apply. " André Breton, demoralizing the old psychic processes by the destruction of logic, has discovered a world of magic in the study of the dream via the Freudian explorations, and he has insisted on expressing those interior currents with new words or word associations.

Miss Gertrude Stein attempts to find a mysticism of the word by the process of thought thinking itself. She does not deform the word as such, but gives it new sensations by giving it its mathematical power. Of late she has been trying to develop a new sense of grammar.

Verbal neologisms were first attempted in Germany by August Stramm. Here is one of his poems:

Abendgang

Durch schmiege Nacht
Schweigt unser Schritt dahin
Die Haende bangen blass um krampfes Grauen
Der Schein sticht scharf in Schatten unser Haupt
In Schatten
Uns!
Hoch flimmt der Stern

Die Pappel haengt herauf
Und
Hebt die Erde nach
Die schlafe Erde armt den nackten Himmel
Du schaust und schauerst
Deine Lippen duensten
Der Himmel kuesst
Und
Uns gebaert der Kuss!

While Stramm limited himself to the problem of re-recreating nouns as verbs and adjectives, Hans Arp, who is really a Frenchman, played havoc with the lyric mind by inventing word combinations set against a fantastic ideology.

Certain others went so far as to reproduce gestures only by word symbols. These, however, remained mostly sound paroxysms. Very little can be said also for the futuristic theory of " words in liberty." It did not solve the problem, since it ignored the psychic contents of poetry. Because a work of art is primarily a vision expressed through rhythm, Marinetti's idea, insisting on movement as the sole criterion of expression, remains abortive.

James Joyce has independently found his solution. The texture of his neologies is based on a huge synthesis. There is a logic of his own back of every innovation. The root of his evolution can be traced to *Ulysses*. There, already, Mr. Joyce contemplated the disintegration of words. In the interior monologue words became disjointed from their traditional arrangements, and new possibilities for timbre and associations were discovered. In developing his medium to the fullest, Mr. Joyce is after all doing only what Shakespeare has done in his later plays, such as *The Winter's Tale*

and *Cymbeline,* where the playwright obviously embarked
on new word sensations before reaching that haven of peace-
fulness mirrored in the final benediction speech from the
latter play which closes the strife of tongues in *Ulysses.*
Let us consider, for example, the following quotations
from *Cymbeline,* selected at random throughout the play.

Sec. Gent. You speak him far
First Gent. I do extend him, sir, within himself ;
Crush him together, rather than unfold
His measure duly.

Imo.   Thou shouldst have made him
As little as a crow, or less, ere left
To after-eye him.
Pis.   Madam, so I did.
Imo. I would have broke mine eye-strings ; crack'd them, but
To look upon him ; till the diminution
Of space had pointed him sharp as my needle.

Imo. What is the matter, trow ?
Iach.   The cloyed will,
That satiate yet unsatisfied desire, that tub
Both fill'd and running, ravening first the lamb,
Longs after for the garbage.

Post. ....
'Tis still a dream ; or else such stuff as madmen
Tongue, and brain not : ....

Iach. ....
For beauty that made barren the swell'd boast

Of him that best could speak; for feature, laming
The shrine of Venus, or straight-pight Minerva,
Postures beyond brief nature; for condition,
A shop of all the qualities that man
Loves woman for; besides, that hook of wiving,
Fairness which strikes the eye,

Post. ....   Then began
a stop i' the chaser, a retire; anon
A rout, confusion-thick: forthwith they fly
Chickens, the way which they stoop'd eagles; slaves,
The strides they victors made: and now our cowards,
Like fragments in hard voyages, became
The life o' the need: ....

In connection with this last quotation, it is interesting to
compare the effect of haste and confusion of the battle with
a similar passage from Work in Progress, the description of
the Battle of Waterloo in the opening pages.

" This is lipoleums in the rowdy howses. This is the Willingdone, by the splinters of Cork, order fire. Tonnerre! (Bullsear!
Play!) This is camelry, this is floodens, this is panickburns. This
is Willingdone cry. Brum! Brum! Cumbrum! This is jinnies
cry. Underwetter! Ghoat strip Finnlambs! This is jinnies rinn-
ing away dowan a bunkersheels. With a trip on a trip on a trip on
a trip so airy, etc. "

Then there are the coinages of words to be found in
Cymbeline such as, " cravens ", " after-eye ", " imperceive-
rant ", " straight-pight ", " chaffless ", " whoreson ",
" under-peep ", " wrying ", etc.
Needless to say, had Shakespeare employed precisely the
same innovations as Mr. Joyce, the quarrel would have long

since died down, Mr. Joyce's course to-day would be plain sailing and his role that of the imitator rather than the innovator. In all the examples cited, however, there is an easily recognizable analogy in the very personal, almost obscure intention of the artist, which makes no concessions to communication other than a tantalizing invitation to the reader to seek and continue to seek, if he would know the complete thought behind earth phrase ; and in Joyce's work there are at least bits of recognizable drift-wood floating on the surface of the stream, which is not the case in the Shakespeare quotations, where the reader's cue lies deep and well hidden under the word flow.

James Joyce gives his words odors and sounds that the conventional standard does not know. In his super-temporal and super-spatial composition, language is being born anew before our eyes. Each chapter has an internal rhythm differentiated in proportion to the contents. The words are compressed into stark, blasting accents. They have the tempo of the Liffey itself flowing to the sea. Everything that the world of appearance shows, everything that the automatic life shows, interests him in relation to the huge philosophic and linguistic pattern he has undertaken. The human element across his words becomes the passive agent of some strange and inescapable destiny.

Those who have heard Mr. Joyce read aloud from *Work in Progress* know the immense rhythmic beauty of his technique. It has a musical flow that flatters the ear, that has the organic structure of works of nature, that transmits painstakingly every vowel and consonant formed by his ear. Reading aloud the following excerpt may give an idea of this :

" Shall we follow each others a steplonger whiles our liege

is taking his refreshment ? There grew up beside you amid our orisons of the speediest in Novena Lodge, Novara Avenue, in fltwaspriduum-am-Bummel oaf, outofwork, one removed from an unwashed savage, on his keeping and in yours, that other, Immaculatus, that pure one, he who was well known to celestine circles before he sped aloft, a chum of the angels, a youth they so tickerly wanted as gamefellow that they asked his mother for little earps brupper to let him tome to Tintertarten, pease, and hing his scooter 'long and 'tend they were all real brothers in the big justright home where Dodd lives, that mother smothered model, that goodlooker with not a flaw whose spiritual toilettes were the talk of half the town, and him you laid low with one hand one fine May in the Meddle of your Might, your bosom foe (not one did you slay, no, but a continent!), to find out how his innard worked !"

The English language, because of its universality, seems particularly fitted for a re-birth along the lines envisaged by Mr. Joyce. His word formations and deformations spring from more than a dozen foreign languages. Taking as his physical background the languages spoken in the British Empire, past and present (Afrikaans-Dutch : South-Africa ; French : Canada; etc.) he has created a language of a certain bewilderment, to be sure, but of a new richness and power for those who are willing to enter into the spirit of it. Even modern American, so fertile in astonishing anarchic properties, has been used by him. The spontaneous flux of his style is aided by his idea to disregard the norms of orthodox syntax. Using the pun, Mr. Joyce has succeeded in giving us numerous felicitous *tournures* in spite of the jeers of the professors. Did not the New Testament itself use puns in order to put over an idea ? " Tu es Petrus, et super hanc petrum aedificabo ecclesiam meam," which is used in the first book, provides certainly a sufficiently good precedent.

For it is the condition between waking and sleeping as well as sleep itself which James Joyce is presenting to us in his monumental work. Here for the first time in any literature, the attempt is successfully made to describe that huge world of dreams, that a-logical sequence of events remembered or inhibited, that universe of demoniacal humor and magic which has seemed impenetrable so far. (To be sure, Gerhardt Hauptmann in *Hannele's Himmelfahrt* attempted to present a dream-state, but it remained bound in the old literary conceptions as far as the actual expression was concerned). The dynamics of the sleep-mind is here presented with an imagination that has whirled together all the past, present and future, as well as every space related to human and inorganic evolution.

But in developing this theme, Joyce realized that the elements of sleep have never been properly described as far as the real night language is concerned. Obviously we do not use the same words while asleep as those we employ when awake. If you make the experiment of transcribing the narrative events of your dream, you will forever be confronted with this difficulty. Every writer who has tried to communicate his dreams to us has stumbled against the inadequacy of his presentational or verbal medium. For the broken images of the dream floating through a distorted film and the actual mechanics of words that occur in the movement need a radically new attitude.

James Joyce has given us this solution, and his language corresponds to this need. Listen to " Father Viking Sleeps," the physiological description of sleep in *Work in progress*:

" Liverpoor? Sot a bit of it! His braynes coolt parritch,

his pelt nassy, his heart's adrone, his bluidstreams acrawl, his puff but a piff, his extremeties extremely so Humph is in his doge. Words weigh no more to him than raindrips to Rothfernhim. Which we all like. Rain. When we sleep. Drops. But wait until our sleeping. Drain. Sdops "

I DONT KNOW WHAT TO CALL IT BUT ITS MIGHTY UNLIKE PROSE

BY

VICTOR LLONA

I DONT KNOW WHAT TO CALL IT BUT ITS MIGHTY UNLIKE PROSE

BY

Victor LLONA.

Among so many other things, what we have seen so far of *Work in Progress* appears to be a « divertissement philologique », if I may borrow the pat expression of a lover of such entertainments, M. Valery Larbaud. A glittering, mysterious show, ringing with laughter, yet somber, poetic, and fundamentally sad, like all the spectacles born of an artist's disenchanted brains.

A vast company of actorwords — not only of the English, but of many languages, both dead and alive — cavort here in a whirlwind dramatic ballet to a polyphonic orchestral accompaniment, while the eyes of the audience are dazzled and soothed in turns by a display of colours which runs the gamut of a lavish palette. Each one a character in costume — some recognizable at first sight, others inscrutable in a novel garb, perhaps a wilful deformation of their lawful vestment — these words skip and prance, shout, lisp, sing or speak their lines, flit like birds of ravishing or disconcerting plumage in and out of the purposely darkened stage, while multicoloured beams of light play intermittently upon the boards flashing upon a fragmentary scene, disclosing a stiff tableau vivant, or affording a glimpse of some sprightly cavalier seul suspended in mid-air, only to turn away from him at once, so that we shall never know whether the bold performer did land upon his feet or break his neck at the end of his pirouette.

To increase our mystification, the virtuoso stage director sends in at times his words by pairs or trios, so interlocked and arbitrarily matched, that we are puzzled at first, as though we saw some three-headed monster, never before beheld. We scrutinize the phenomenon, level our lorgnettes, crane our necks and peer at the freaks. Why, it's only a German root sandwiched in between two stolid English monosyllables, or perhaps a vagrant Portuguese noun marshalled up for our judgment between two French gendarmes.

*
* *

To venture an opinion on the other aspects of Mr. Joyce's latest work would be premature. Yet those aspects no doubt are the essential ones. The problem of style, for instance. One cannot help but feel that this new work will advance the technique of writing far beyond the point where it has been marking time since the publication of *Ulysses*. Another aspect is the mode of presentation of the story — or rather of the prose epic. Another yet the fine restraint with which a stupendous erudition is made use of to give colour, body and perspective without ever being allowed to intrude purely as encyclopaedic matter — a true miracle of artistry.

Whatever may be the ultimate scope of the work — possibly a panoramic view of human story — the fragments we have so far are gigantic. Given the perfectly balanced craftsmanship of Mr. Joyce, the size and density of the parts are a sure indication as to the proportions of the whole.

* *

The handling of language by Mr. Joyce presents such obvious innovations, that it has drawn the attention of the critics almost to the exclusion of all the other features of his new work. Here criticism is entirely permissible, for surely the clues we have so far may serve to give us an insight into what is to follow.

The embodiment of foreign words into a given language is by no means a new departure. The practice has been, and still is, resorted to, both spontaneously by the people and deliberately by the writers, especially at such times when the language has reached a point in its development where it must be fashioned into a literary vehicle, or when it sorely needs rejuvenating. In other words, both when the language is born to artistic expression, and when it has to be given, artificially, a fresh lease of life.

But never was the procedure indulged in on such a scale, with such determination — so radically, in such a revolutionary manner.

* *

Rabelais, to whom Mr. Joyce bears much more than a surface likeness, did it. The father of French prose literally coined hundreds of neologisms, of which an astounding number are still heartily alive. A proof that language *can* be made by a writer [1].

1. Cf. for their similarity and difference Rabelais' account of the siege of Corinth by Philip of Macedon (book III, prologue): " Les ungs, des champs

98

On the other hand, in order to coin his neologisms, Rabelais drew mostly from Latin and from Greek — a little (vicariously) from Hebrew and Arabic — but I have never seen an instance when he forged compound words made up of foreign roots or syllables pieced together with roots and fragments of French words — which seems to be the most startling innovation in Mr. Joyce's handling of the English language.

Rabelais' daring never went so far as that. Perhaps this artifice never occurred to him. Perhaps there were other reasons for this reticence on the part of one who dared so much. First of all, the author of *Gargantua* was French and used French, his own language by right of birth, for which he had perhaps a much greater reverence than Mr. Joyce, an Irishman of revolutionary tendencies (in literature, at least), could possibly entertain for the King's English. Another — and perhaps weightier — reason, is that the French tongue, at the time Rabelais used it, was still in the formative period. It was a sturdy infant — as sturdy a baby as Gargantua himself — not the worn out methuselah we have with us today.

es forteresses retiroyent meubles, bestail, grains, vins, fruictz ", and so on, an account itmpedimented with military baggage from several |plundered languages, with the description of the Great Dublin Duke (Cf. the account of the battle of Waterloo, Transition I, p. 14) : " This is the big Sraughter Willingdone, grand and magentic in his goldtin spurs and his ironed dux and his quarterbrass woodysyhoes and his magnate's gharters and his bangkok's best and goliar's goloshes and his pulloponeasyan wartrews. " Where the hero stands horsed under a seven cubit " arc de triomphe en ciel " signed by words of power and battle.

In a Life of Rabelais which the writer of this essay is now preparing, he endeavours to analyse in detail this fascinating subject of the literary, imaginative and suggestive handling of language in metamorphosis or in a transitional stage — a problem which today is as urgent as it was in Rabelaïs' age.

Consequently no such drastic innovations were required to give life and zest to Rabelais' vehicle of expression.

To these reasons may be added a third. Prof. Sainéan, in his enlightening work, *Le Langage de Rabelais,* has proved beyond discussion that Maistre Françoys really knew very little of the foreign languages of his day.

" What strikes one ", he says, " when perusing the novel, is the great number of idioms which are met with therein. Some enthusiastic commentators have made of Rabelais the greatest polyglot of the Renaissance.

" This judgment must be toned down. This polyglottism is but a purely literary contrivance. Our author really knew only the classical tongues (Latin and Greek) and Italian. He had but a pretty superficial smattering of Hebrew, and knew nothing, like everybody else in his time, of Arabic and Spanish, as well as of the idioms which are encountered here and there in his work. "

In this respect Mr. Joyce is far more learned than Rabelais. His knowledge of foreign languages is as diversified as it is sound. Italian he speaks like a native. German and French he knows as well. He has better than a working practice in Spanish, Portuguese, Dutch and the Scandinavian languages. Words of seventeen tongues have been identified so far in his new work — and every one of them is used with a surety of touch that bespeaks more than a nodding acquaintance.

Yet what judgment may one pass on this widespread weaving of extraneous threads into the fundamental language of a literary work? Does not the author take the erudition of his readers too much for granted? Perhaps he does not care. To quote Stendhal's " mot " in his *Foreword* to *The Memoirs of a Tourist* :

" Mr. L..., accustomed as he was to speak Spanish and

English in the colonies, had admitted many words of those tongues (into his writing) as being more expressive.

" 'Expressive ! no doubt', I said to him, 'but only for those who know Spanish and English.' "

Here Stendhal talks like one of those pests, so numerous among his countrymen, " les hommes de bon sens ". Nonetheless the crux of the matter is there. Mr. Joyce expects too much from his readers. Few, if any, will possess the knowledge of languages — and other sciences — that would allow them fully to grasp the niceties of meaning in this work.

However, he may point out, were he disposed to answer such criticism, that in this departure he but anticipates the trend of the times, which assuredly leans to a thorough internationalization in speech as in everything else. The world today is not the restricted, insular province that it still was in Stendhal's time. The prodigious development of the means of locomotion and of the means for spreading thought has brought about a radical change in this provincialism, not to mention the upheaval of the War, the like of which had never been seen in the world on such a scale since the Barbaric invasions which marked the close of the Roman Empire.

*
* *

When completed, no doubt, *Work in Progress* will still prove a hard nut to crack for the vast majority of its readers. Mr. Joyce will suscitate a host of commentators who may in some respects smooth the way for the vulgum pecus. These scholars, as is their wont, will fight and squabble over "obscure " passages, draw up glossaries and indulge in longwinded dissertations as to the esoteric meaning of certain fragments. But Rabelais was sufficiently understood during his life-time, for he had launched his giants into a world of true and tried readers. France, in the 16th century, contained, I am sure, a greater proportion of educated men capable of following him upon the roughest paths, than is the case among the English-speaking public from whom Mr. Joyce must expect to muster his followers.

Such commentators, however, would have tickled the risible faculties of Rabelais enormously. I hope that Mr. Joyce will live long enough to enjoy the fun of which his literary forbear was so unfortunately deprived, for I suspect that the commentaries of future critics of his new work will not lack in amusing elements.

We would be better inspired if we made an honest effort and tried to see the light by ourselves. Here and there I glimpse in *Work in Progress* certain gleams, furtive and fleeting, I perceive certain recurring sounds which might give a key to the secret. Thus in a kaleidoscope, the fragments of coloured glass which form the apparently endless patterns are few — and in each fresh and unexpected pattern, we end by identifying the constituting elements, detecting thus the rhythm of the successive pictures. The work still in progress might be of such design, and the difficulties it offers might be less than it appears at first sight.

Mr. Joyce may have a surprise in store for us. His artistry is so consummate that he may bring order out of apparent chaos by a mere literary artifice. Up to the present, the fragments that have appeared suggest the disordered, illogical imagery of dreams, the babblings and mutterings of human beings upon the brink of sleep. The dreamers may awake and talk coherently — after their visions during slumber have served to give us an insight into their subconscious souls.

These blurred speeches, moreover, may be intended to represent the Past.

I feel that with the last fragments shall come the revelation.

* *

To me, one of the most striking and illuminating thing in connection with *Work in Progress* is that it has managed to reverse the consecrated order of things. We commentators simply could not be kept in leash — we had to have our say in a volume which will grace the stalls in advance of the text under consideration.

I should like to be told of another example of this out of the history of literature.

Mr. JOYCE DIRECTS
AN IRISH WORD BALLET

BY

ROBERT McALMON

Mr. JOYCE DIRECTS
AN IRISH WORD BALLET

BY

Robert McAlmon.

In a period post-dating the admission of the subconscious
as important to individual and general human destinies, and
when an acceptance of relativity forces the realization that
facts and ideas are neither as hard nor as logical as some
minds wish them, it is natural that a literature should
emerge which is evocative rather than explanatory, more
intent upon composite types, plots, and situations, than on
particularized meanings. Had the inhabitants of the tower of
Babel sought for an esperanto language, their gropings would
have been, to be successful, into some composite subconscious
of individual and race types; the language emerging might
readily have been a dance or a symphony of music, with
whatever evocations and implications the movements of a
ballet or the combinations of sound summoned to any
particular subconscious. The ability to respond to suggestion
varies greatly. However, music and the ballet are less
inhibited by the demands of *meaning* than literature has
been. Audiences do not insist upon a story or a situation to
appreciate the movements of a dance or the strains of music.
Critics allow that there can be a pure art in these mediums;

they have sometimes come to permit with painting, sculpturing and architecture, that for evoking a pleasurable emotion or sensation, form and colour does not have to be utilitarian, descriptive, literal, or possessed of *meaning* other than the intent to awaken response

Also good comedy, clowning, pantomine, nonsense, slapstick, drollery, does not appeal to the sense of humour by explanation, but by gesture. In such good dances or music as are humorous, it is rarely possible to define the reasons for the comic appeal. Prose too can possess the gesticulative quality.

In Ulysses James Joyce made a summary of a good share of the failure of the entire christian era. Whether it was his purpose or not, and it probably was not his intent, he damned intellectually the religious and metaphysical logics of Jesuitism, emphatically, and of Christianity as a whole, generally, for the effects they had on him and his race and his realization of what they have done to the emotions of people. Having what has been called his " detestable genius " for words, their intonations, connotations, and rhythms, he often achieved orchestral effects with his prose, but the morale underlying the book was such that it suited too perfectly the morale of the time when it first appeared. Then, four years after the war the world had come to an end ; there was an end ; there had to be a new beginning ; and Joyce, realizing *since years* that minds to not think in sentences, that the subconscious does not think or feel in ideas, but in images, and these images not consecutive or related to our as yet unscientific understanding of psychology, surely wished to break though language to give it greater flexibility and nuance. To him language does not mean the English language ; it means a medium capable of suggestion, implication, and evocation ;

a medium as free as any art medium should be, and as the dance at its best can be. Primitive tribes, particularly the Indians of North America, know sign language as a means of communications ; African tribes, by drums, dances, and a variety of gestures get their emotions across without the necessary means of a common language. Isadora Duncan's dream of a dancing America, of masses of dancing figures, of a populace released to fuller realizations because permitted to express themselves individually in a mass, no one much questions because she is dealing with the dance. As yet literature is unfreed, because to most people it is bound up with the idea of story telling, the drama of single lives or a group of lives. It still is under the shadow of medieval philosophies, religion, and reasoning, to such an extent that its scope is limited. Joyce, one judges, wishes to evolve a prose that deals with human types, mytholgies, eruditions, and languages, compositely.

In Anna Livia Plurabelle, which is written to suggest the flowing of the river, it is hardly important that Mr. Joyce has with great pains sought the names of all rivers on earth and 8 in hell, and heaven. Unless the satisfaction he himself gets matters enough so that it transmits a satisfaction to the reader, it does not appear significant that he sought for the word *peace* in 29 languages so that he might call a composite female character *peace* in 29 ways ; and similarly with *twilight* that after much research he finds that in the Burmese there is only the word Nyi-ako-mah-thi-ta-thi, which translates literally into " the time when younger brother meets elder brother, does not recognize him but yet recognizes him ". What is important is the sensations evoked, the sensibilities made susceptible to response, by his writing, and that necessarily varies with each individual reader. The question " but what

does it all mean " need not be asked; it means variously, to
Joyce himself and to each reader, as a Mozart, or a Beethoven
or a Strawinsky symphony means variously to different people
and variously to the same persons in various moods and
circumstances. Generally the new work in Progress with
which Mr. Joyce is now occupied is sprinkled with classical
allusions ; he may, at the time of writing, find a particular
passage that suggests to him a classical mythological figure,
a reminiscence of Dublin, an ironical crack at the works and
pomps of catholicism, a sentimental thought about some
loved person of his present or past acquaintance, and again
a memory of Dublin. Dublin he cannot forget ;

" What was thaas ? Fog was whaas ? Too mult sleepth.
Let sleepth.

" But really now whenabouts. Expatiate then how much
times we live in. Yes ?

" So not by night by naught by naket, in those good old
lousy days gone by, the days, shall we say ? of whom shall
we say ? while kinderwardens minded their twinsbed, there-
now theystood, the sycomores, all four of them, at their
pussy-corners, and their old time pallyollogass playing copers
fearsome, with Gus Walker, the cuddy, and his poor old
dying boosy cough. esker, Newcsele, Saggard, Crumlin, Dell
me, Donk, the way to Wumblin, Follow me beeline and
you're Bumblin, Esker, Newscle, Saggard, Crumlin, and
listening, so gladied up when nicechild kevin Mary (who
was going to be commandeering chief of the choirboys' brigade
the moment he grew up under all the auspices). Irishsmiled
in his milky way of cream dwibble and onage tustard and des-
sed tabbage, frighted out when badbrat Jerry Goldophing (who
was hurrying to be cardinal scullion in a night refuge as soon
as he was cured enough under all the hospitals) furrinfrow-

ned down his wrinkly waste of methlated spirits ick and lemoncholy lees ick and pulverised rhubarbarorum icky. "

What the above passage means to Joyce I cannot say.   To
me it means that he cannot forget Dublin, cannot forget
schooldays, and childhood.   To a Dubliner it would mean
possibly more; but to me childhood memories, nightfears and
humours, weeping willows rather than sycamores, and a hac-
kingly coughing consumptive town drunkard are evoked, and
the suggestion of male pedagogues, monitors in a wet-the-bed
ward of a boarding school.   He is not doing characterizations
of definite characters ; he is implying the being and having
been of types that are general to all times and places, and
according to the readers background do the composite characters suggested take on feature.   He cannot forget Dublin, and
in his Irish tenor prose lemoncholy way he must sing or be
mumbling a Dublin Irish come-all-you in a wistful twilight
remembering occasionally Greece and her myths such as a
barber whispering to the rushes that Midas has golden ears,
or recalling that the twilight of madness descended on Swift.

" Unslow, malswift, pro mean, proh noblesse, Atrahore,
melancolores, nears ; whose glauque eves glitt bedimmed to
imm ; whose fingrings creep o'er skull : till quench., asterr mist
calls estarr and graw, honath Jon raves homes glowcoma. "

Inevitably swift madness (bad swiftness) mean and noble
the black hour black care sits behind the horseman (bringing
near) melancholy (black coloured sorrow) ; whose owlsighted
green eyes glimpse of reason or sight, bedimmed and bedam-
med by the fingers of incipient dementia creep o'er the skull
(crepuscle); till one star (asterr : Greek) in being quenched
names another star wench, estarr (German for blindness) and
graue (starr) (greenstar, glaucoma) grauestarr, cataract, grey,
shwarsz starr, for black and the dissolution of the retina.

But also, for Joyce, asterr is one of his composite female characters, Esther Johnson, and Estarr is Hester Vanhomrigh, and probably he thought of Astarte, as he thought with *graw* of his glaucoma, approaching blindness, grey love is cold, he remembers his love for words, for the quality which is onomatopoeic. And Honath Jon raves in a delirium of dreams for the homes of the star women, Stella and Vanessa, in this passage compositely suggested by *quench*, their homes suggesting fireside and repose, the glow coma of repose.

It is unlikely that Joyce himself understands from a re-reading of his present writing all that he thought it had in the way of implication. So much as he is dealing with prose for the evocative capacities which it possesses his psychology and mythology are the renderings of his subconscious in the hope of reaching an audience that responds pleasurably to the implications of his involved orchestral theme. In the above quoted passage the emotional impact of its *meaning* could be the painful record of a subconscious quivering with terrors as in a night crise, but by using the english language only as a basis, while weaving in classic mythology, German, latin, and French, words or rythms, he has managed to depersonalize his emotions and situations sufficiently to take the raw quivering of a suffering spirit out of the passage. This manner he utilizes frequently. There is no telling what languages he is using if one is not a person who knows eighty languages and well. The extent of his erudition is wide, but not so great as people sometimes assume it to be. He admits to philological " ragpicking " because the great passion of his life is words, their colours and implications ; he does not intend to create a new literary esperanto, but he wishes to originate a flexible language that might be an esperanto of the subconscious and he wishes to believe that anybody reading his work gets a sensation of understanding, which is the understanding which music is allowed without too much explanation. His readers who take him with least effort are probably the younger generation, who have grown up with machinery, the radio, the aeroplane, with psycholanalysis enough accepted as a progressing study so that fewer laymen swallow it hook and sinker, with relativity a theory that can be accepted for the timebeing as was Newton's in the past. This generation may demand less explanation about the meaning of meaning. Being well out of the period when there was much argument about abstract art, cubisms, futurisms, and pure form, they may without bewilderment and resentment, permit their sensibilities to remain open and susceptible and capable of response to the implications of a literature that is not a literature of escape, of interpretation, of propaganda or reform, or of God or morality seeking. In Joyce are the backgrounds of his race, his education, his subconscious and conscious responses to mythology, poetry, metaphysics that are mainly Jesuit, and from the source of his subconscious flows the stream of his wish to evoke literary music, a ballet of dancing words that suggest the clear line and mass form which is the beauty quality that good art has. The river may be flowing, or he may be wishing to summon up the sounds of night or to awaken the emotions that night thoughts bring. The symbol of the river flowing however is not the important factor; it can be too insularly insisted upon to the extent of limiting the capacities for stimulating the reader's sensual-sensitive esthetic response to prose music; and more, what to Joyce the sounds of a river flowing evokes emotionally may be quite other than the effect of riverflowing sounds upon another person. But what these sounds bring into his operating conscious from the scource of his subconscious can have gratifying implications for that other person never-theless. The Irish tenor prose sings on, deriving from classic literature and mythology and religion. The stream of the sub-conscious reveals itself, derived also from the sources, (always mainly Dublinesque), of folklore and folksong, of Celtic bards, of Celtic legends of slim maidens with dark hair and lithe bodies and breasts, of laughter and the continual melan-choly plaint of Celtic whimsy, fatalism, and the erratic shift of mood. Church music sounds here, and the half remem-bered refrain of a sentimental ballad of the 90's breaks in to be itself broken in upon by a barroom ballad or the ribald refrain of a bawdy house song. Limericks are woven into the Irish tenor wailings. No more than Joyce can forget Dublin and Jesuitism and Irish homelife and family can he resist his mania for playing with words and phrases, punning. The gossip of housewives is suggested; the chatter of lounging, lazy, shiftless barroom and streetcorner politicians plays through the prose. The preachings and moralizings of priests, washerwomen, and parents, is woven into the pattern with ironic taunts against pedantries and the manners of editorial and newspaper writings ; the insistence upon the Dublin-a-male-city with a woman either a respectable woman or a bloody whore is less in this new work than it was in Ulysses, and to that extent is older and more resigned. He cares less now for ideas and situations except as a basis for using the medium of prose as a medium for declaring his passion for words and their suggestions.

In an as yet unpublished portion of the new work this is a passage with a definite situation, but with the characters composite, and in time without age, but of course the scene must be Dublin since Joyce cannot forgive Dublin and the Dublin of 1904, which was when he left it for the last time.

A time.
Act : Dumbshow.
Closeup.

Man with nightcap, in bed, fore. Woman. With Curl-
pins, hind. Discovered. Side point of view. First position
of harmony. Say: Eh ? Ha. Check action. Matt. Male
partly masking female. Man looking round, beastly expression, fishy eyes, exhibits rage. Business. Ruddy blond-
beer wig, gross build, episcopolian, any age, Woman, sit-
ting, looks at ceiling, haggish expression, peaky nose, exhibits
fear. Welshrabbit tint, turfi tuft, undersized, free kirk.
No age. Closeup. Play.
Cry off. Her move.
You have here Joyce's intentness on making his characters
and his effects a composite evocation, of types, or of the sum-
marization of a kind of poetry sensation, movement, or a spe-
cies of act. In the rest of the scene nothing happens but the
Joycian conversation between the man and woman, man and
wife, and the crying of one of their two little boys. Jean qui
Rit and Jean qui Pleure. The woman goes to comfort the
weeping little boy. The man follows her to the hallway to
look on secretively. The mother, comforting the boy.
" You were dreamed, dear. The pawdrag ? The faw-
thrig ? Shoe. Hear are no phanthares in the room at all.
No bad faathern, dear one. Opop opap capallo, muy malin-
chily malchick. Gothgored father dowon followay tomollow
the lucky load to Lublin for make his thoroughbass gross-
man's bigness. Take that two pieces big slap slap bold
honty bottomside pap pap pappa.

Li ne dormis ?
— S ; Malbone dormas.

Kial li Krias nokte ?
Parolas infanete.   S.

Sonly all in your imagination, dim.   Poor little brittle magic nation, dim of mind.   Shoe to me now, dear.   Shoom
of me.   While elvery stream winds seling on for to keep this
barrel of bounty rolling. ''

Here Joyce cannot forget childhood, parenthood, mother
affection and anxiety, but most of all he cannot forget Dublin,
Lublin, the memory of a Dublin folksong punned at and
joked with, the lucky load to Lublin, the wage-earning father,
and Ireland, poor brittle little magic nation, dim of mind.
Ireland, little Jean qui Pleure, with Joyce crooning an Irish
tenor twilight refrain to comfort the weeping child who awakes in fright from having had a bad nightmare.   The mother
does not call little Jean a melancholy bad little chick.   Joyce
is playing with language, English, Russian, and latin, in this
passage.   The refrain of mother to child is all comforting, as
Joyce sees it, but after a time he sees he has given it other
implications.   Gothgored father, perhaps a priest is praying
as the mother tells of the no bad faathern, dear one, who goes
the lucky load to Lublin for to make the family groceries,
while every silvery stream (elvery) winds sailing selling (seling) on to keep the barrel of bounty rolling.

It is possibly necessary to '' trance '' oneself into a state of
word intoxication, flitting-concept inebriation, to enjoy this
work to the fullest.   Surely the author himself has written in
a state of exaltation, where the mood is witty, comic, or glim-
mery tragic, according to the passage ; but the mood is only
indicated rather than stated, defined, and dwellingly insisted
upon.   Whether Anna Livia is being a lithesome, taunting,
woodnymph of an irish lass, or a garrulous knotty old wash

woman, she is in the process of representing womankind, the femalenesses of life ; and old man river, as a randy young buck or as a rutty, fibrous, eternally impregnating aged male, is representing the masculinities ; and the two are composites, not only of humanity, sexes, bi- , heter, and what have you, but there is the attempt to suggest through the ebb and flow of the prose the possibilities and relativities inherent in existence.

To what extent the imaginary being, the common man, or the common reader, can get a pleasurable sensation out of reading this work, is difficult to say ; but if there is such a being as the common man, he probably does not read much, except detective tales or housemaid romances or the sporting news. He probably does not care much for the dance in ballet form and disassociated from sex and story telling ; his response to music is likely to be of the sort that what he is accustomed to he believes he likes. But that common man, if a simple and not too complex but healthily curious minded man might be more capable than the precious esthete or critic of responding to the evocative and suggestive quality of a literature. That imaginary " common man " may not have been educated away from ability to respond directly, through having learned academically what is art, or beauty, or style. The common man ought to be as receptive as a sensitive child, but try and find him. In general it is not unlikely that Mr. Joyce in his new work in progress summons too insistently and often the wonder emotions, the religious emotions, that have in them presentments of death, intonations of fear and despair, or a humour that is too mainly Dublin masculine and Irish teasings. That however is his race quality ; he has not escaped the twilight, nor the church ; he is still summing up an age which some people believe past and too allied to the medieval age of hampering gods, prejudices, and unscientific attitudes. Surely, nevertheless he has broken into language and made it a medium much freer, more sensitive, musical and flexible, while retaining a subject content still meaty with psychologic, historic, and sociologic comprehensions. He has become freed in a manner of metaphysical pomposities such as dominated the ideas, religions, and apprehensions of many great talents of the Past. He has always been free of the need to give messages to the world and his fellowmen ; and it is his intentness upon his love for words which has given him this freedom, very probably.

THE CATHOLIC
ELEMENT IN *WORK IN PROGRESS*

BY

THOMAS McGREEVY

THE CATHOLIC
ELEMENT IN *WORK IN PROGRESS*

BY

Thomas McGreevy

The technique of Mr. Joyce's *Work in Progress* has probably been already sufficiently explained to give readers interested in serious literature a line of approach to it. Technique is, of course, important always and there are still technical aspects of the work the implications of which will continue to interest the critic. It seems to me, for instance, to be noteworthy as marking not a reaction from realism but the carrying on of realism to the point where it breaks of its own volition into fantasy, into the verbal materials of which realism, unknown to the realists, partly consisted. This fantasy is obviously richer than the fantasy of, say, Mr. Walter de la Mare, which turns away from reality and takes refuge in a childishness which at its best is no more than charming. Perhaps the best justification for the technique of *Work in Progress*, however, was that implied in the phrase of the late President of the English Royal Academy of Art at the 1928 Academy Banquet in London (See *The Observer*, May 6, 1928). " There are ", he said, " examples in our language so perfect in their beauty and fitness that one feels they cannot have been formed out of a language already fixed but that a language had been created in order that they may emerge. " I do not know whether Sir Frank Dicksee had *Work in Progress* in mind when he was speaking. I scarcely think it likely. But evidently he might have. For Mr. Joyce has created a language that is necessary precisely to give beauty and fitness to his new work.

It is well to remember, however, that the beauty and fitness are the important things and technical considerations may be put aside for a moment in order to consider *Work In Progress* from the point of view of other beauties and fitnesses than verbal ones. Obviously, the book being still unfinished, one may not yet say that it is marked by beauty and fitness as a whole. But every chapter and passage that has appeared is so admirably realised and so related to every other chapter and passage that one has no doubts that when the end does come the author of *Ulysses* will have justified himself again as a prose writer who combines a wellnigh flawless sense of the significance of words with a power to construct on a scale scarcely equalled in English literature since the Renaissance, not even by the author of *Paradise Lost*. The splendour of order, to use Saint Thomas's phrase, has not been the dominating characteristic of modern English prose and it is partly because the quality was demonstrated on a vast scale in *Ulysses* that that book marked a literary revolution. And signs are not absent that, in spite of the difficulty of having to invent a new language as he writes, Mr. Joyce in his latest work has lost nothing of his amazing power in this direction.

That the conception of the story as a whole is influenced by the *Purgatorio* and still more by the philosophy of Vico is well known. Mr. Joyce is a traditionalist, a classicist.

That is why he is regarded as a revolutionary not only by the academic critics but by those of the fervidly scientific advanced school whose attitude towards the biology of words is not what, if they were consistent, they ought to wish it to be. The deep-rooted Catholicism of *Ulysses* was what most upset the pastiche Catholicism of many fashionable critics in England. The enthusiastic converts who discover the surface beauties of Catholicism at the older universities, ·" temporary " Catholics one might call them, tend always to be shocked by the more profound " regular " Catholicism of Ireland. And one remembers the difficulties of even the true born English Catholic Bishop Ullathorne in trying to keep the over enthusiastic converts Newman and Manning in order. To an intelligent Irishman and to Mr. Joyce least of all, Catholicism is never a matter of standing on one leg. It is not a pose, it is fundamental. Consequently it has to face everything.

But the temporary Romanizers were as shocked by the unsavoury element in *Ulysses* as a sentimental Saracen of the middle ages might have been by the way in which Dante put popes in hell (compare, incidentally, the introduction of the phantoms of the Catholic and Church of Ireland primates into the night-town scene in *Ulysses*). Again Irish Catholics are not shocked by finding amongst the detail in the superb monogram page (*Christi autem generatio*) of the Book of Kells two rats tearing the Host from each other with their teeth. They face the fact, as the monk who painted the page faced it, that devilry exists. The *Introibo ad altare diaboli* with its response *To the devil which hath made glad my young days* intoned by Father Malachi O'Flynn and The Reverend Mr. Love in *Ulysses* should be taken in exactly the same spirit as the rats in the work of the monk. But an

English Catholic critic writing of *Ulysses* wanted it all to be like the passage relating to the chanting of the Creed :

The proud potent titles clanged over Stephen's memory the triumph of their brazen bells : *et unam sanctam catholicam et apostolicam ecclesiam* ; the slow growth and change of rite and dogma like his own rare thoughts, a chemistry of stars. Symbol of the Apostles in the Mass for Pope Marcellus, the voices blended, singing alone aloud in affirmation : and behind their chant the vigilant angel of the church militant disarmed and menaced her heresiarchs. A horde of heresies fleeing with mitres awry : Photius and the brood of mockers and Arius, warring his life long upon the consubstantiality of the Son with the Father and Valentine spurning Christ's terrene body and the subtle heresiarch Sabellius who held that the Father was Himself His own Son ..... idle mockery. The void awaits surely all them that weave the wind : a menace, a disarming and a worsting from those embattled angels of the Church, Michael's host who defend her ever in the hour of conflict with their lances and shields.

He went on glibly to say, " it is a case of *corruptio optimi pessima* and a great Jesuit-trained talent has gone over malignantly and mockingly to the powers of evil ". He presumably rejects and would eliminate the rats from the Book of Kells, the gargoyles from the thirteenth century cathedrals of all Europe.

Actually, it is worth while to note, malignance and mockery are precisely the things that are absent in *Ulysses*. In this inferno from which Stephen is ever trying spiritually to escape, for he, unlike the Jewish Bloom, knows the distinction between the law of nature and the law of grace and is in revolt against the former however unable he be to realise the latter even the most obscene characters are viewed with a Dantesque detachment that must inevitably shock the inquisitorially minded.   These do not notice that as Stephen leaves after having put out the light on the scene that revolted him by smashing the chandelier the Voice of All the Blessed is heard calling:

Alleluia, for the Lord God Omnipotent reigneth!

The inquisitorially minded I hasten to add however, exist in Ireland as well as in England.   We in Ireland have been, though only to a relatively slight extent, affected, first during the Penal times when our priests had to be educated abroad, by French Jansenism and the orientally fanatical Catholicism of Spain and later during the nineteenth century by our political association with the censorious Nonconformity of England.   We are even now founding an Inquisition in Dublin though one may believe that it is not likely to be a very successful obstacle to the self-expression of a people who with fewer pretensions have a sense of a larger tradition than that of the half-educated suburbans who initiated the idea of a new censorship.   These latter understand no more than the enthusiastic converts who lay down the law to nobler men than themselves in England that Catholicism in litera-ture has never been merely lady-like and that when a really great Catholic writer sets out to create an inferno it will be an inferno.   For Ulysses is an inferno.   As Homer sent his Ulysses wandering through an inferno of Greek mythology and Virgil his Aeneas through one of Roman mythology so Dante himself voyaged through the inferno of the mediaeval Christian imagination and so Mr. Joyce sent his hero through the inferno of modern subjectivity.   The values are not altered but because Mr. Joyce is a great realist it is the most real of all — one notes for instance that the Voice of All the Damned is the Voice of All the Blessed reversed, a realistic and understandable effect (c. f. Dante's mysterious and not altogether intelligible " *Pape Satan, pape Satan aleppe...* ") — and it is as terrible and pitiful as any.

The purgatorial aspect of *Work in Progress* is most obvious, of course, in the purgatorial, transitional language in which it is written. This language is adequate to the theme. Purgatory is not fixed and static like the four last things, death, judgment, heaven and hell. The people there are not as rooted in evil — or, for Dante or for Mr. Joyce, even in personality — as the people in the inferno. And therefore for literary purposes, not in definitive language either. In *Work in Progress* the characters speak a language made up of scraps of half the languages known to mankind. Passing through a state of flux or transition they catch at every verbal, every syllabic, association. Is it not natural that in such circumstances without irreverence — on the contrary indeed — *Qui Tecum vivit et regnat* should become for one of them *Quick takeum whiffat and drainit* and that *In the name of the Father and of the Son and of the Holy Ghost* should become *In the name of the former and of the latter and of their holocaust*. The former is surely the Eternal, the latter the world and the holocaust the world consumed by fire as pre-ordained from eternity.

Then there is a politically purgatorial side to the work dominated by the figure, intermediate from every point of view, of the Anglo-Irishman, Earwigger, Persse O'Reilley. And there is, perhaps, the personal purgatory of the author. I imagine — though it is an interpretation of my own that the writer himself is suggested in that transitional stage of self-realisation when he was still James Joyce the musician who, to find himself finally as an artist, had to become James Joyce the writer. All through his work it is evident that

Mr. Joyce never loses sight of the fact that the principality of hell and the state of purgatory are in life and by the law of nature not less within us than the kingdom of heaven. The questions of the law of grace triumphant and of a modern Paradiso will probably be more appropriately raised in some years' time.

Vico is the imaginative philosopher, the Dante, of the Counter Reformation, little known though there is a road bearing the Neapolitan name in Norwegian Dalkey, a suburb of Dublin. The conception at the back of *Work in Progress* is influenced by the Vico theory of the four stages of human society's evolution. But the working out of the parallel between the Vico conception and the reconstruction of it in regarding Dublin's life history in *Work in Progress* must wait till the complete work has appeared. The thunder clap, in Vico's system, the most dramatic manifestation to primitive man of a supreme, incalculable being is there in Part I, however, and students of Vico will be able as the work moves, to completion to recognise the second third and fourth of the Neapolitan's main ideas, marriage according to the auspices, the burial of the dead and divine providence in the other parts of it. They may be taken as comically foreshadowed in the childish sing-song repeated in one of the chapters that have already appeared, " Harry me, marry me, bury me, bind me ".

Coming thus to less vast considerations there are details of the work which, in their beauty and fitness are unsurpassed even by the finest things in Ulysses. As characters, the mysterious viking father of Dublin — Dublin was founded by the " Danes " — and his hustru (woman of the house), the wayward Anna Livia, the river Liffey, Dublin's mother, stand out above all, in some ways more than any of the whole gallery of amazing figures in the earlier work, but the

Pecksniffian Earwicker, protean and purgatorial, though less epic is not less vivid. Then there is that broth-of-a-boy Siegmund-Shaun, sometimes figuring as a cherub, sometimes imagining himself a priest, a much more muscular type of Christian than Stephen Daedalus, entirely uninfluenced by Greek or Judaistic thought, the burliest Norse-Irish convert who ever escaladed the walls of Maynooth. As for verbal beauties and fitnesses there are passages and phrases all through that have the delicate magic and dramatic force that one takes so much for granted from Mr. Joyce simply because he is Mr. Joyce. There is the first paragraph of all with the voice of Brigid answering from the turf fire, *mishe! mishe!* (I am, I am) to *tauf tauf* (baptise!) *thuartpeatrick* (peat, Patrick). There is the final passage from the Anna Livia chapter when the two women are discovered as tree and stone ; there is the paragraph at the beginning of Part III beginning, " Methought as I was dropping asleep in somepart in nonland of where's please " and the other " When lo! (whish o whish) mesaw, mestreamed through deafths of durkness I heard a voice. " There is the meditation on the death of Mrs. Sanders to compare with an earlier Dublin meditation (Swift's on the death of Hester) and the delicious little story ot the Ondt and the Gracehoper [1] (the champions of space and time respectively) told by Shaun immediately afterwards. The portrait of the Ondt is worth reproducing.

He was a weltall fellow, raumybult and abelboobied, bynear saw altitudinous wee a schelling in kopfers. He was sair sair sullemn and chairmanlooking when he was not making spaces in his psyche, but laus! when he wore making spaces

1. Republished in *Three Fragments from Work in Progress,* Black Sun Press, Paris.

on his ikey he ware mouche moore secred and wisechairman-looking.

This little interpolation is a satire but it is satire that is like all good satire intensely serious and it is subjected to the discipline of literary form.   There is much talk of Time in it — see for instance the passage describing the saturnalian funeral of the old earwig (here transformed into Besterfarther zeuts) piously arranged by the Gracehoper to an accompaniment of planetary music :

The whool of the whaal in the wheel of the whorl of the Boubou from Bourneum has thus come to town.

Much, perhaps all, art consists in seeing the funeral of one's past from the emotionally static point of artistic creation — emotion recollected in tranquility — time recollected in space.   The London master of spaces should read Mr. Joyce's fable.   He might learn from it that Gracehopers, for all their seeming time-ness are much more in space than the Ondts who decide that they will " not come to party at that lopps ". The author of *Time and the Western Man* is a writer of remarkable potentialities but he has so much contempt for time that he never takes enough time to finish anything properly.   If he would read the story of the Ondt and the Gracehoper, not impatiently but patiently he might learn from it how to write satire not like a barbarian, ineffectively but like an artist, effectively.

MR JOYCE'S TREATMENT OF PLOT

BY

ELLIOT PAUL

MR. JOYCE'S TREATMENT
OF PLOT

BY

Elliot PAUL.

Since the first book, or part, of Mr. Joyce's work was completed in *transition*, and is available for study as a whole, it is now possible to consider his general plan and discuss such of his innovations as are more fundamental and original than the distortion and combination of words and the blending into an English composition of languages bordering upon English. Naturally, with small fragments only before the critic, the philological aspect of the work has attracted the principal attention. Strangely enough, Mr. Joyce has almost universally been denied the right to do on a larger scale what any Yankee foreman employing foreign laborers does habitually on a smaller scale, namely, to work out a more elastic and a richer vocabulary which will serve purposes unserved by school-room English.

This is not the only strange thing about the reception of this work. With the precedent of *Ulysses* to suggest that Joyce is capable of construction in the grand manner, the majority of his former supporters have blandly assumed that the present book is confused and meaningless and that he is wasting his genius beyond the legitimate area within which an artist may move.

There are so many men whose gifts and trainings would make them so much better able to interpret Mr. Joyce's work than I am, that I offer the following observations with heartfelt timidity. Had all such men come forward, this article would have been unnecessary. But how few have found either time or inclination to do so. My own inadequacy may, perhaps, afford them encouragement.

In the first place, it seems futile to compare the new work with any other book, especially *Ulysses*. There is no similarity, either in execution or intent. Many indications aside from the fact that the book begins in the middle of a sentence point out that its design is circular, without the beginning, middle and ending prescribed for chronological narratives. The idea of past, present and future must be laid aside, if one is to grasp the composition.

This is not impossible, given the slightest familiarity with modern developments in physics or mathematics or even a moderate appreciation of recent tendencies in painting. If one can consider all events as having a standing regardless of date, that the happenings of all the years are taken from their place on the shelf and arranged, not in numerical order, but according to a design dictated by the mind of Joyce, then the text is not nearly so puzzling. For example, if Noah, Premier Gladstone and " Papa " Browning are telescoped into one, because of common characteristics, no violence is done to logic.

" Take an old geeser who calls on his skirt. Note his sleek hair, so elegant, *tableau vivant*. He vows her to be his own honey-lamb, swears they will be papa pals, by Sam, and share good times way down west in a guaranteed happy lovenest when May moon she shines and they twit twinkle all the night, combing the comet's tail up right and shooting popguns at the stars. For dear old grumpapar, he's gone on the razzledar, through gazing and crazing and blazing at the stars. She wants her wardrobe to hear from above by return with cash so as she can buy her Peter Robinson trousseau and cut a dash with Arty, Bert or possibly Charley Chance (who knows?) so toll oll Mr. Hunker you're too dada for me to dance (so off she goes!) and that's how half the gels in town has got their bottom drars while grumpapar he's trying to hitch his braces on to his trars. But old grum he's not so clean dippy between sweet you and yum (not on your life, boy! not in those trousers! not by a large jugful!) for someplace on the sly, old grum has his gel number two (bravevow, our Grum!) and he would like to canoodle her too some part of the time for he is downright fond of his number one but O he's fair mashed on peaches number two so that if he could only canoodle the two all three would feel genuinely happy, it's as simple as A. B. C., the two mixers, we mean, with their cherrybun chappy (for he is simply shamming dippy) if they all were afloat in a dreamlifeboat, hugging two by two in his zoo-doo-you-doo, a tofftoff for thee, missymissy for me and howcameyouse'enso for Farber, in his tippy, upindown dippy, tiptoptippy canoodle, can you?"

The treatment of space is equally elastic. Phoenix Park, Dublin, becomes interchangeable at one time with the Garden of Eden, again with the Biblical universe. The Wellington monument and the surrounding drill-field contains the field of Waterloo, when the author is so minded. Mr. Joyce takes a point of view which commands all the seas and continents and the clouds enveloping the earth. In one chapter Anna Liffey, which represents Eve and the multi-monikered feminine element of the book, is joined to more than fourhundred rivers by name and reference, including the four rivers of Paradise and the four infernal rivers.

The characters are composed of hundreds of legendary and historical figures, as the incidents are derived from countless events. The " hero " or principal male character is primarily Adam, and includes Abraham, Isaac, Noah, Napoleon, the Archangel Michael, Saint Patrick, Jesse James, any one at all who may be considered " the big man " in any given situation. He is called each of the separate names by which he has been known, or more frequently H. C. E. (Here Comes Everybody, H. C. Earwicker). His symbol in nature is the mountain.

His female counterpart, the river, is Eve, Josephine, Isolde, Sarah, Aimee MacPherson, whoever you like occupying the role of leading lady at any time or place. She is called most often Anna Livia.

The philosophical framework upon which the text is draped was suggested to Mr. Joyce by a page from Vico, an Italian philosopher of the late seventeenth century, who proves to his own satisfaction the existence of a higher power from the evidence in history that each new civilization in turn finds in the ruins of its successor the elements necessary for its growth. Vico likens civilization to the Phoenix. Joyce stages his cosmos in Phoenix Park.

The " elements " of the plot, which are not strung out, one after the other, but are organized in such a way that any phrase may serve as a part of more than one of them, are taken from stories which are familiar to almost any one. Among these are the fall of man in the Garden of Eden. From beginning to end, a discussion of the nature of the original sin is carried on in undertones, and often comes directly to the surface. The tale of Noah's ark, culminating with the rainbow as a symbol of God's promise recurs again and again, and the seven colors of the spectrum, thinly disguised, crop out in frequent passages. " the old terror of the dames, came hip hop handihap out through the pikeopened arkway of his three shuttoned castles, in his broadginger hat and his civic chollar and his allabuff hemmed, like a rudd yellan gruebleen orangeman in his violet indignonation ".

The " fall motif " is easily discerned in the Ballad of Persse O'Reilley combined with the original sin inquest :

> " He was joulting by Wellinton's monument
> Our rotorious hippopopotamuns
> When some bugger let down the backtrap of the omnibus
> And he caught his death of fusiliers "

The installment contained in *transition*. No. 6 contains a detailed treatment, numbered and in order of their importance, of the twelve principal elements which are not concerned with plot, but with characters, location, etc., of the book. The first is H. C. E, the second Anna Livia, the third their home, the fourth the garden, the fifth the manservant, the sixth the maidservant, and so on.

The conflict between Michael and Lucifer is one of the " plot elements " which can be traced through almost any page. The fable of the " Mookse and the Gripes " is a good starting point for the study of this component part, although it appears in the first installment " O foenix culprit! Ex nickylow malo comes mickelmassed bonum, etc. " Variations of the Latin phrase " O felix culpa " (which surely will puzzle no Catholic) occur frequently,

The battle of Waterloo, with Wellington and Napoleon substituting for Michael and Nick, is not an impossible leap for an agile imagination, and the fact that Phoenix Park is dominated by the Wellington monument makes these parallel trains of ideas quite easy to follow.

The Irish ballad of Finnegan's wake serves as a vehicle for the Humpty Dumpty and the fall of Satan stories in several instances. Finnegan was an Irish contractor who fell from a scaffolding and was stretched out for dead. When his friends toasted him at the supposed wake, Finnegan, aroused by the word " whiskey ", sat up and drank. (The word " usque-adbaugham" is a variant of the Gaelic for whiskey.)

The birth of Isaac, the legend of Finn MacCool, the murder of Abel by Cane, the Tristan and Isolde story, numerous other familiar legends are similarly employed in the pattern of Mr. Joyce's book, and the design must be considered three dimensionally. Often, in a painting, a part of the canvas contains several forms, one in front of another, with the near ones transparent, So must one of Mr. Joyce's paragraphs be understood. He has achieved actual polyphony, far beyond the implied polyphony of the Cyclops chapter of Ulysses, for example.

I have made no attempt to say all that may be said about his treatment of plot. If I have given a cue as to how to proceed in the delightful exercise of discovering it and enjoying it, I shall be quite content. Those who cannot transcend Aristotle need make no attempt to read this fascinating epic. The ideas do not march single file, nor at a uniform speed.

Whatever difficulties the individual words may present, and they have been much exaggerated, — however baffling it may be to find the elements of character and of plot extending forward and backward as well as from left to right, the sentence structure and the syntax generally will offer no obstacles. Although sentences are frequently long, their lines are definite and the parent ideas stand head and shoulders above their flock of details. Gems like the following are inconspicuous only because of the equal excellence of their context:

" Lead kindly foul! They always did: ask the ages. What bird has done yesterday man may do next year, be it fly, be it moult, be it hatch, be it agreement in the nest. For her socioscientific sense is sound as a bell, sir, her volucrine automutativeness right on normalcy: she knows, she just feels she was kind of born to lay and love eggs (trust her to propagate the speccies and hoosh her fluffballs safe through din an danger!); lastly but mostly, in her genesic field it is all game and no gammon, she is ladylike en everything she does and plays the gentleman's part every time. Let us auspice it! Yes, before all this has time to end the golden age must return with its vengeance. Man will become dirigible, age will be rejuvenated, woman with her ridiculous white burden will reach by one step sublime incubation, the manewanting human lioness with her dishorned discipular manram will lie down together publicly flank upon fleece. No, assuredly, they are not justified, those gloompourers, who grouse that letters have never been quite their old selves again since that weird weekday in bleak Janiveer when, to the shock of both, Biddy Doran looked at literature. "

It is to be expected that Mr. Joyce's enormous and incidental contribution to philology will be recognized in advance of his subtler aesthetic achievements but the latter is sure to follow and it may prove interesting to observe how, one by one, his former supporters try to creep unostentatiously over the tailboard of the bandwagon.

JOYCE & HIS DYNAMIC

BY

JOHN RODKER

JOYCE & HIS DYNAMIC

BY

John RODKER.

With this latest work some enquiry into the symbols that govern the communication through writing of thought and emotion becomes imperative. It would seem that we have reached a degree of consciousness where we find it no longer adequate to use words as we use them in speeeh, for we recognise in speech only the superficial movement of profounder currents.

How do men then, through literature, communicate with each other and what is it they succeed in conveying.

Certainly they use words and these words and the meanings commonly attached to them, provoke in the reader associations true for himself, possibly widely true for humanity, but it may be remote in the extreme from the author's intention. In any case the accustomed channels traced by speech and the writing that resembles it provoke no confusion, no complication of associations. They may be said to follow the path of least resistance ; least resistance for the author, least resistance in the reader, no transfusion, no change.

Yet the reader is susceptible to contacts profounder than those described, indeed he commonly supplies them to complete the author's indications which for a multitude of reasons the author has found himself unable or unwilling to fill in. Here it is as though the words held in solution the elements, inarticulate in both reader and author, which we call dynamic; their core is those basic preoccupations round which we most deeply move, they are at the root of every later development of the soul; these have always been the chief preoccupation and gratification of what we call creative writing. For thinking is first affective, words make it flesh in so far as they serve to define feeling, but beneath all words lie affective contacts which might, it would seem, entirely dispense with words as signs but not as sounds.

Not only is this so but any word, however unjustifiable and nonsensical it may seem, moves the mind to an attempt to visualise that word. The new term borrows from and consequently lends to the term it apes, the abortive associations which accompany it cannot but enrich with their frustrated vibrations the term which was the basis of the invention. This is an extreme instance interesting only as an example of how the mind works, but it must be obvious that an author, completely aware (and by completely I mean to a degree transcending literature as we have known it) of the forces he is using and anxious to produce the most naturalistic picture possible of an individual and of the repressions, complications, forces which direct that individual before they express themselves in words, must have recourse to all the hybrid formless onomatopoeic and conventional sounds in which feeling clothes itself[1].

1. A consideration (notion, idea) or an idea is *relevant* to an interpretation when it forms part of the psychological context which links other contexts together in the peculiar fashion in which interpretation so links them. Irrel-

Should his technique then be adequate to all these requirements he will most quickly and vitally establish himself (on
his own terms and not on those of his auditor) in a permanent
symbiosis with that auditor.

Joyce's virtuosity in this new work is a very remarkable
phenomenon in that it is adequate to the requirements post-
ulated. Because of his method, because of his pursuit of the
innumerable paths of association by means of all the word —
ways capable of delimiting them, if not exactly, at least with
a precision so far unknown in literature, he now brings to
fruition what was foreshadowed in Ulysses ; the possibility of
a complete symbiosis of reader and writer ; the only obstacle
which now remains being the inadequacy of the reader's
sphere of reference — not to the emotional content — but to
the ideas, objects and events given.

Yet when Ulysses made its first appearance it seemed incomprehensible to a number of people. It is a complaint we
do not at all hear today. Evidently then, though in a somewhat unusual and baffling form, the elements which composed it were well within the sphere of contemporary reference.

The dynamic aspect of the work derives a large part of its
importance from the fact that words are used so to speak 'in
vacuo' by means of which they still preserve much of their
ancient magic. Puns, klang words, mantrams are powerful
because they are disguised manifestations of revengeful and
iconoclastic impulses driven underground by fear ; and be-

evant consideration is a non-linking member of a psychological context...
mental process is not determined purely psychologically but by blood pressure
also.

The Meaning of Meaning. C. K. Ogden and I. A. Richards.
Kegan Paul.

cause the violence of childhood inspires them, their underground life compacted, made sly, imparts to them an intense vitality.

To show still more obviously that he is creating a language the author indulges in an amazing virtuosity of puns. The child's seeming innocence is to him and to us one of the deepest sources of gratification. Joyce makes intense use of this screen.

How sly satire can prove, how joyful, how inspiring, what lusts of combat it can evoke let the parable of the Mookse and the Gripes or the immense Rabelaisian humour of the 5th 'transition' instalment witness.

The need for a vehicle by means of which to express the more elaborate consciousness of the time provoked, I imagine, the apparition of a Rabelais and Chaucer. To formal expression, formal emotion, they opposed their individualities and the vitality of common speech, which by its nature is not subject to the refinements which seem inevitably to accompany the development of literature and the spread of writing.

Since the vernacular is as it were a storehouse of all the sounds necessary to expression, however complicatedly foreign or refined they may seem today in regard to the actual needs of the populace, the common speech holds within it relics of tongues spoken it may be millions of years before symbols were invented. It is impossible therefore for us not to respond to words, all words and all forms of words, but writing and speech are so denatured that it is important, if we are not forever to be deprived of part of our emotional inheritance, that these primitive forms be returned to us. Joyce is doing this for us; the result is an intense and basic revitalising of words and our attitude to them. Posterity is immensely indebted to him.

We see for ourselves in the Europe of today that there has been little which by the standards we know but find so hard to define, can be called dynamic. Emotion iu literature has grown formal, as have perhaps the emotions themselves, and it is very apparent how the writer's consciousness seems continually to grow more circumscribed.

Joyce is revitalising our language in a form which borrows vastly from the past in its every protean disguise. In the vernacular, whether English, Irish, American or any of the combinations of these or other tongues, he finds that breath which will revivify our dying tongue. Is not this perhaps the most important aspect of his work? And is it not already predestined to be — with its content — a mine where future writers will quarry as they are already quarrying in Ulysses; a pyramid of language, a monument to time built with such loving care, so great a feeling for material, such density, as to be unique in English.

This work also contains psychological implications of the greatest value and has been created with a concentration of toil which must be unique among the writers of this generation.

As to its meaning?

As in the unconscious, in this new work there is no time. Events, people, make their own relevant conjunctions. Events are people too, a whole cosmographication of them. But the form is so elusive — alas where is our field of reference — and the associations often so personal to the author as to be incomprehensible to us that it seems half the matter is lost, as though indeed it were the inside of a pyramid which must always be hidden from us.

Is it possible this attempt to make the unconscious conscious may but end in confusing the *rapport* between author and reader ? Possibly for a while. But a first confusion gives place to a deeper, more complete identification ; and I think of Ulysses and how with the complete work and some passage of time this « Work in Progress » must become apparent to us.

This is certain. « Work in Progress » is much in advance of Ulysses, both as to elasticity of writing, naturalism, the pulse of life ; it is technically unique, as Ulysses was not. In the straight passages, such as those concerned with the River Liffey, no writer to my knowledge, drawing from all the sources of human comparison has ever rendered so rapturously, so indirectly, or so revealingly (it is not strange that the secret, the baffled should be to us more profoundly, dynamically true than the simple) the life of a river — river of life ; nor elsewhere evoked such moments of inarticulate rapture.

BEFORE *ULYSSES* — AND AFTER

BY

ROBERT SAGE

BEFORE *ULYSSES* — AND AFTER

Robert SAGE.

The general bafflement caused by those portions of James Joyce's *Work in Progress* which have appeared in *transition* seems to me an indication that most readers have failed to realize that Joyce's writings, from *Dubliners* to the present book, form an indivisible whole.

Ordinarily the graph of a writer's career ascends, with slight irregularities, to a horizontal line representing the culmination of development. That is, after a period of trial and error, he achieves an individual manner of expression and his works thenceforth are variations on a theme, becoming successively richer perhaps and more perfect but not differing in their bases one from another.

Joyce's development, conversely, has been and continues to be a firm mounting line. Each of his books has represented an enormous advance in expression and technique, each has been the record of a corresponding advance in the author's spiritual life. It is unlikely that he will repeat himself ; and to predict, as some have done, that he will in the end return to the simplicity of *Dubliners* is to admit a profound incomprehension of his mind.

This consistent development is apparent even in single books, as may be noticed by comparing the first pages of

A Portrait of the Artist as a Young Man with the closing
pages or the first chapter of *Ulysses* with the ensuing ones.
But, like other writers, Joyce has of course his constant qualities, although they are less evident ; and it is these that must
be searched for in his earlier works before a proper approach
may be made to *Work in Progress*.

The progression through *Dubliners,* the *Portrait* and *Ulysses* to the present work, besides demonstrating a steady spiritual and literary expansion, crystallizes one constant factor
that is of primary importance in understanding Joyce ; namely,
the fact that his style and technique are tyrannically dictated
by the nature of his subject.   In this respect his writing is
perhaps the purest in the English language.   There is a strong
personal dye in all that he has ever written, from an unpre-
tentious phrase in *Chamber Music* to an involved page-long
sentence in *Work in Progress* ; but the elasticity and resilience
of his technique are so immense that they permit it to stretch
out and close in over every minute tendril of the subject's
organism, whereas in the works of other writers the corners
and protruding ends are apt to be chipped off in order that
the main portions may be crammed into the confines of a
rigid technique.   It is this power that sometimes makes Joyce
difficult, for, since the subject is so closely encased, there
remain none of the vacant spaces which another writer would
fill in with explanations.

In *A Portrait of the Artist as a Young Man* the narrative
opens in the babbling language and from the irrational viewpoint of a small child.   As the child grows older the language
and viewpoint become imperceptibly riper in proportion, until
the story ultimately takes the form of the entries which
Stephen Dedalus makes in his diary when his soul is tortured
by the mental and physical revolt of adolescence.   Nothing

outside the consciousness of Stephen is included nor is there a phrase in the novel which does not contribute directly to the development of the theme.

The vantage point of *Ulysses*, a vastly more complex book, in which the subconscious to a large extent supplants the external and the conscious, shifts frequently, yet the rhythm, the tempo, the vocabulary and the limits of the frame are always determined by the subject.

The consistency with which Joyce adheres to this method is illustrated too by his disdain for transitions. When one unit of his work has come to its natural termination he drops it and turns to the next. He does not insert an announcement that six months have now passed in the life of Stephen or that the ensuing pages will reproduce the drowsy flow of Mrs Bloom's consciousness as she lies in bed. Such a procedure would be alien to his mind and would seriously damage the organic quality of his writing.

This closeness of composition is intimately related to another phase of Joyce's character — his preoccupation with words, a preoccupation which, apparent in the verbal precision of his early writing, has now become so highly developed that it has blinded most of his readers to the rich internal art of his latest work.

On the first page of the first story in *Dubliners* (written when Joyce was in his early twenties) I find the following significant passage :

" Every night as I gazed up at the window I said softly to myself the word paralysis. It had always sounded strangely in my ears, like the word gnomon in the Euclid and the word simony in the Catechism. But now it sounded to me like the name of some maleficent and sinful being. It filled me with fear, and yet I longed to be nearer to it and to look upon its deadly work. "

His readers will remember Stephen's reflections after discussing the word *funnel* with the dean of his school, an English convert to Catholicism :

" — The language in which we are speaking is his before it is mine. How different are the words *home, Christ, ale, master,* on his lips and on mine! I cannot speak or write these words without unrest of spirit. His language, so familiar and so foreign, will always be for me an acquired speech. I have not made or accepted its words. My voice holds them at bay. My soul frets in the shadow of his language. "

Again, the youthful Stephen communes with himself as he stands on the North Bull bridge :

" He drew forth a phrase from his treasure and spoke it softly to himself :
" — A day of dappled seaborne clouds.
" The phrase and the day and the scene harmonized in a chord. Words. Was it their colours ? He allowed them to glow and fade, hue after hue : sunrise gold, the russet and green of apple orchards, azure of waves, the greyfringed fleece of clouds. No, it was not their colours : it was the poise and balance of the period itself. Did he then love the rhythmic rise and fall of words better than their associations of legend and colour ? Or was it that, being as weak of sight as he was shy of mind, he drew less pleasure from the reflection of the glowing sensible world through the prism of a language many-coloured and richly storied than from the contemplation of an inner world of individual emotions mirrored perfectly in a lucid supple periodic prose ? "

Here is Stephen-Joyce reacting to the occult power of words as another might react to caresses or blows. His " soul frets " in their presence, they " fill him with fear ", certain of them he " cannot speak or write without unrest of spirit ", they evoke in him more intense emotions than the phenomena of the outer world. This is not an affectation. It is as vital a part of Joyce as his Irish birth or his Catholic training. Possibly, as he suggests, the weakness of his eyesight has sensitized his appreciation of the images that may be built from words ; but, whatever the cause, this almost abnormal need for the nourishment of verbal associations has made it possible for him to write such sentences as " And low stole o'er the stillness the heartbeats of sleep ", in which he voices an emotion tuned to the pulse of the ages and familiar to all humankind.

It is little wonder then that, as the years have gone by, Joyce has reached out farther and farther in his explorations of the world's languages and has cut ever more deeply into the roots of the language formed by the successive generations of his ancestors. Nor is it any wonder that the wealth and range of his vocabulary have grown with each chapter and that his interests in recent years have become concentrated on the magnificent universe that may be brought into being by language.

It may at first seem that a chasm as wide as infinity separates the warm melodious lines above quoted from such sentences as :

" So you need hardly spell me how every word will be bound ove to carry three score and ten toptypsical reading throughout the book of Doublends Jined till Death, who oped it, closeth thereof the dor. "

But each passage comes in its time. The Joyce of today is reflected as authentically in the last quotation as was the adolescent Stephen in the verses he wrote when " the liquid letters of speech, symbols of the element of mystery, flowed forth over his brain ".

Inevitably his extension of the boundaries of language has been but half of the phenomenon which is complemented by a similar enlargement of conception. By following Joyce's evolution through the four prose works one finds his " inner world of individual emotions " widening out from the intensely personal until it circumscribes a crowded cosmography. The short stories of *Dubliners* were re-creations of people Joyce had known in Dublin and of events he had witnessed. Beyond this, the stories were rich in personal and atmospheric overtones, but it was not until he wrote the *Portrait* that he was to subordinate the visible world. Here, despite the superb characterization of Simon Dedalus and such graphic scenes as the Christmas dinner, he was occupied with his own spiritual self, in recording the *de profundis* of a sensitive boy's turbulent passage through the sexual and spiritual crises of adolescence. *Ulysses* in parts ascended to a cosmic plane and displayed a Joyce who had advanced from the spiritual conflicts of youth to the more complex ones of maturity. Individual emotions were now tranformed into the universal. Leopold Bloom and Stephen Dedalus, for all the realistic cataloguing of their thoughts, actions and habits, were phases of Joyce's mind personified by figures similar in dimension to Pantagruel, Faust or Don Quixotte. Dublin, although its streets, pubs, shops and citizens were called by name, was not so much the insular capital of 300,000 inhabitants as it was a universal city freed from all geographical boundaries. The acute consciousness that formed the roadway through the *Portrait* was frequently abandoned for explorations in the pits of the unconscious.

It can be seen today that there already existed most of the indications of what Joyce would do next, not only in the universalization of character and scene but in the accompanying technical and philological inventions. But it is extremely doubtful that even his closest students predicted the enormous distance he was to travel between the completion of *Ulysses* in 1921 and the publication of the opening pages of *Work in Progress* in *transition* six years later.

Yet his direction has continued to be in a straight line : his new work is intimately associated with what he has done in the past and its origins are to be found in his earlier books. *Work in Progress* again takes the form decreed by the conception, it again demonstrates Joyce's preoccupation with the word and his mastery of it, it is again the transformation of a troubled spirit into the symbols of social life, it again makes use of the necessary technical inventions, it carries to the extreme limits the universalization of character and the sketching of a cosmorama started in *Ulysses*, and, like all of Joyce's books, it is again fundamentally a book of Dublin.

It is all this and much more — but always within the limits of that straight line. This time Joyce enlarges upon his method of reproducing the synthetic creations of half-consciousness, which he introduced so remarkably in the closing pages of *Ulysses*, and carries it to the realm of sleep, where thousands of thoughts are thrown together into a pattern expressed by a vocabulary of its own. He has embraced the world, heaven, hell and the celestial bodies, and, instead or observing the traditional chronological scheme, with the narrative fibres sharply separated and treated as individual unities, he has telescoped time, space, all humanity and the universe of gods and heroes. This latter fact — consistent with his own development but in opposition to all previous literary canons — should be emphasized in order that the uninitiated reader will understand at the outset that he is faced with a revolutionary four-dimensional conception of the universe, that the

" characters " who bob up briefly, disappear and reappear in various forms and in unexpected company are composite, that time plays no part, that Joyce reaches out into all space to take what he for the moment requires. The reader must be prepared at times to visualize several related images simultaneously, realizing that these images are not necessarily bound together by surface-obvious associational chains but that their range may include any desired point in political or religious history, legend, fable, mythology, science, mathematics, current events, etc.

In this unprecedented creative work there is, properly speaking, no plot, no character development, no action, no narrative sequence. Instead there is presented such a picture of the entire universe as might be registered in the slumbering mind of a capricious god who, from some infinite point in space, had witnessed the planets and heaven and hell unwind their history on the edge of those few terrestrial square miles now known by the name of Dublin.

History, as we all know, is none too reliable; but the purpose, at least, of the modern historian is to record, correlate and interpret facts as accurately as possible. The Biblical, Greek and Celtic historians, however, were hindered by no such prosaic idea. The Bible is a hodgepodge of fact and legend. Ancient Greek history is so tightly bound up with the feats of the gods that myth and actuality are inseparably merged. The early chroniclers of Ireland told their history mostly through colorful legends. And anyone with a true appreciation of the art of storytelling will prefer these old histories where facts are buried within imaginative stories to the new histories which are dry catalogues of dates and events; for the former offer truth through the medium of art and the latter only reach an approximate truth through research and reporting.

Coming from a country as rich in legend and folklore as Ireland, it is not surprising that Joyce should have had the idea of *creating* a history of the universe and creating a language in which such a history would have to be related. This, in brief, is what he has done in the book that at present is known only as *Work in Progress*. On a cosmic scale it is the history of Dublin and the spiritual and intellectual autobiography of Joyce. Figures of the past and present flit through it spectrally as they have through the world's existence and through the mind of Joyce. Finn MacCool, Adam and Eve, Humpty-Dumpty, Napoleon, Daddy Browning, Lucifer, Wyndham Lewis, the Archangel Michael, Santa Claus, Tristram and Isolde, Noah, St. Patrick, Thor and Dean Swift are a few of the thousands of worthies whose shades pass through the pages of *Work in Progress*.

All this is indicated by Joyce himself, who says on page 16 of *transition* no. 5 :

" The proteiform graph itself is a polyhedron of scripture. There was a time when naif alphabetters would have written it down the tracing of a purely deliquescent recidivist, possibly ambidextrous, snubnosed probably and presenting a strangely profound rainbowl in his (or her) occiput   Closer inspection of the *bordereau* would reveal a multiplicity of personalities inflicted on the document and some prevision of virtual crime or crimes might be made by anyone unwary enough before any suitable occasion for it or them had so far managed to happen along.   In fact, under the close eyes of the inspectors the traits featuring the *chiaroscuro* coalesce, their contrarieties eliminated, in one stable somebody similarly as by the providential warring of heart shaker with housebreaker and of dramdrinker against free thinker our social something bowls along bumpily, experiencing a jolting series of prearranged disappointments, down the long lane of (it's as semper as oxhouse-humper!) generations, more generations and still more generations. "

And a few lines later he offers a bit of advice that may
well be kept in mind while investigating the contents of *Work
in Progress* :

" Now, patience ; and remember patience is the great thing, and
above all things else we must avoid anything like being or becoming
out of patience. "

But even with a general idea of Joyce's purpose and methods,
it is sometimes possible only with difficulty to follow this new
work, for Joyce's erudition results in numerous allusions
outside the usual range of knowledge, while his philological
versatility — often materializing in the obscure form of his
distortions — presents serious obstacles to even his most
sympathetic readers. Moreover, where in the *Portrait* and
Ulysses the abrupt transitions were from chapter to chapter
or from paragraph to paragraph, they are here from sentence
to sentence, from word to word, or even sometimes from syllable to syllable, thus making an unrelieved demand on the
attention.

However, for a closer approach to Joyce's conception, verbal
structure, technique and style, the portions dealing with Anna
Livia are perhaps better adapted to separate consideration
than others, for this theme, while a vital and representative
element of the book as a whole, is self-containing when
detached [1].

Joyce has here immortalized the muddy little River Liffey,
which rises in the Wicklow Mountains about twelve miles
southwest of Dublin and, after curling through some fifty
miles of picturesque scenery, empties into Dublin Bay.

1. Published separately as *Anna Livia Plurabelle,* Crosby Gaige, N. Y.,
1928.

Strangely enough, it differs from the other rivers that have figured in legend and folklore by being personified as a woman instead of a man. Among the sixteen Irish rivers represented by heads on the corners of the old Dublin Customs House the Liffey was the only one with feminine features, and the citizens of Dublin speak affectionately of their miniature river as the Anna Liffey, perhaps taking the name from the old records, where it is referred to as the Avenlithe.

In *Work in Progress* this river is christened Anna Livia, with the Plurabelle added to designate the numerous tiny tributaries of the stream. She becomes neither entirely a woman nor entirely a river, but rather an abstraction, a legendary concept, possessing all the attributes of the female sex and sometimes having the majesty of a goddess, sometimes the shameless promiscuity of a scullery maid. She " coalesces " with other female characters of history, Biblical legend and folklore, returning persistently in one form or another to the surface of the chronicle.

Opposite her is Humphrey Chimpden Earwicker (Here Comes Everybody), the strange composite male character who haunts this cosmic history in many disguises and under endless names, the most frequent of the latter being Persse O'Reilley, a deformation of the word *Perce-Oreille*, the French for " earwig ". He is represented in nature usually by the mountain, and both he and Anna Livia Plurabelle are repeatedly alluded to by their initials or by series of words beginning with these letters.

They are introduced on page 13 of *transition* no. 1 in the following manner :

" Yet may we not see still the brontoichthyan form outlined, aslumbered, even in our own nighttime by the sedge of the troutling stream that Bronto loved and Brunto had a lean on. *Hic cubat edilis*

Apud libertinam parvulam. Whatif she be in flags or flitters, reekierags or sundyechosies, with a mint of monies or beggar a pinnyweight, arrah, sure, we all love little Anny Ruiny, or, we mean to say, love little Anna Rayiny, when unda her brella, mid piddle med puddle she ninnygoes nannygoes nancing by. Yoh! Brontolone slaaps you snoores. Upon Benn Heather, in Seeple Iseut too. The cranic head on him, caster of his reasons, peer yuthner in yondmist. Whooth? His clay feet, swarded in verdigrass, stick up starck where he last fellonem, by the mund of the magazine wall, where our maggy seen all, with her sister-in-shawl. While over against this belles' alliance beyind Ill Sixty, ollollowed ill ! bagsides of the fort, bom, tarabom, tararabom, lurk the ombushes, the site of the liffing-in-wait of the upjock and hockums. "

The passage also illustrates many peculiarities of Joyce's manner, such as the combination of several images in a single word ('' brontoichthyan '' — '' bronto '', thunder: '' ichthyan '', pertaining to fish : '' ichthyol '', brown, the brown liquid made from fossilized fish). The male and female characters are recalled in the initials H. C. E. and A. L. P. of the Latin words. An extraordinary image of the little river's current, vivid and with the non-sense appeal of a nursery rhyme, is evoked in the phonetic effect of the line starting '' mid piddle med puddle '', while Joyce's fondness for puns leads him to place '' maggy seen all '' after a reference to the Magazine wall, the subject of a famous epithet by Swift and one of landmarks of Dublin which is mentioned continually in the work.

Anna Livia's appearance after this is frequent enough, and she entirely occupies the foreground in the closing part of Book I. (The Book of Life), a section which originally appeared in *le Navire d'Argent* of September, 1925, was reprinted in a greatly expanded form in *transition* no. 8 and, after extensive further additions, was issued in a separate volume in the winter of 1928. This portion is beautifully introduced by a passage which immediately precedes it but which is not included in the book ·

" ... with a beck, with a spring, all her rillringlets shaking, rocks drops in her tachie, tramtickets in her hair, all waived to a point and then all innuendation, little oldfashioned mummy, little wonderful mummy, ducking under bridges, bellhopping the weirs, dodging by a bit of bog, rapidshooting round the bends, by Tallaght's green hills and the pools of the phooka and a place they call it Blessington and slipping sly by Sallynoggin, as happy as the day is wet, babbling, bubbling, chattering to herself, deloothering the fields on their elbows leaning with the sloothering slide of her, giddygaddy, grannyma, gossipaceous Anna Livia ! "

Then comes the chatter of two garrulous old washerwomen beating their clothes in the turf-colored waters of the Liffey. " O tell me all about Anna Livia! I want to hear all about Anna Livia. Well, you know Anna Livia? Yes, of course, we all know Anna Livia. Tell me all. Tell me now. You'll die when you hear " — thus starts this episode, written throughout in a rhythmic prose which imitates the sound of the river's current as the banks grow farther apart or approach each other on the course between the mountains and the sea.

The entire episode is the transfigured conversation of the washerwomen prattling scandalously of the things that have been done by the owners of the clothes they are washing. And, as two old women in a village would bring all the townspeople and local events into their gossip, so the washerowmen talk of Dublin, the Dublin of the legendary past, the Dublin of today and the Dublin that existed in the intermediary ages. As night comes on, their voices grow blurred and faint and a metamorphosis takes place, leaving them standing as a stone and an elm tree on the opposite banks of the Liffey.

The real story that lies below the transparent upper plane is that of Anna Livia, Dublin's river, and the sea rover who founded the city. It is the story too of Dublin itself, the Ford of the Hurdles, as brought down from the dim beginning of the ages by record, fable and legend and as kept alive in the speech of its people, the names of its places and the tales passed on by one generation to the next. Or it is, to some extent, the tale of the world's rivers, or even the abstract concept of " river ", for Joyce, giving a new dignity to the pun, has subtly woven into his text the names of hundreds of rivers in all parts of the world, as well as all things possessing fluvial associations.

The characters, as usual, merge : they are Anna and Humphrey, the city and its founder, the river and the mountain, the trout and the salmon, the male and the female — any personnages who conform to the author's purposes. As for the washerwomen whose rambling gossip forms the vehicle for the tale, they, beyond their immediate personalities, are identified in a large sense with the great forces of death and love, which in turn are represented by the immobile stone and the graceful elm.

With this latitude of character treatment, condensation of material and freedom from the restrictions of time and space, Joyce is able to put into the sixty-one small pages of *Anna Livia Plurabelle* a quantity of matter which, elucidatively expanded into a conventional presentation, would fill perhaps several volumes. He once again " covers the subject " by orchestrating his theme with a poetic encyclopaedia of related strains, as in the opening pages of *Work in Progress* he brought together the various versions of the fall motif, from Lucifer to Napoleon and from Humpty-Dumpty to Tim Finnigan.

A multiplicity of concepts placed in immediate contact by a super-rational associational process that is divorced from chronology, place distinction or segregation of fact and myth- and expressed in a special language moulded for their requirements may, then, be taken as the groundwork of Joyce's new book. As Elliot Paul remarked in his essay on its plot elements, the work does not possess the usual beginning, middle and end, but — following Vico's theory of successive civilizations built in a Phoenix-like circle — may begin at any point and end at the same point. *Anna Livia Plurabelle* is a complete unit when read alone, yet its veins and arteries extend to all parts of the organism to which it belongs.

And if *Work in Progress*, because of the magnitude of its subject and the breadth of its treatment, may at first appear to be the most impersonal of Joyce's books, a closer inspection will show that this is an appearance only, for he has found room in these tightly packed pages for the things he has thought, the sights he has seen, the people he has known, the subjects he has read about, the jokes he has heard, the plays he has attended — all the topics that have attracted his interest during a period of many years. Like his unforgettable Leopold Bloom, he is fascinated by the curious and little-known elements of human knowledge; and he has inserted literally thousands of references to these strange subjects in his text, where they blend harmoniously with seemingly foreign neighbors, assuming that universal and timeless sense that makes them collectively form the body of a great new cycle of legends.

It is this unusual manner of working that will cause Joyce's new work to differ from the others in displaying no stylistic advance in its successive pages, for he has, so to speak, written the entire book simultaneously, inserting his new ideas continually in whatever part of the supple text they are appropriate. How *Work in Progress* has developed like a living organism may be observed by a comparison of the three published versions of *Anna Livia Plurabelle*, of which the passage below is a sample:

" Well, you know or don't you know or haven't I told you every story has an end and that's the he and the she of it. Look, look, the dusk is growing. What time is it? It must be late. It's ages now since I or anyone last saw Waterhouse's clock. They took it asunder, I heard them say. When will they reassemble it? "

(Le Navire d'Argent, September, 1925, p. 72.)

" Well, you know or don't you kennet or haven't I told you every story has an end and that's the he and the she of it. Look, look, the dusk is growing. Fieluhr? Filou! What age is it. It saon is late. 'Tis endless now since I or anyone last saw Waterhouse's clock. They took it asunder, I heard them say. When will they reassemble it? "

(Transition, no. 8, p. 33.)

" Well, you know or don't you kennet or haven't I told you every telling has a taling and that's the he and the she of it. Look, look, the dusk is growing. My branches lofty are taking root. And my cold cher's gone ashley. Fieluhr? Filou! What age is at? It saon is late. 'Tis endless now since eye or erewone last saw Waterhouse's clogh. They took it asunder, I hurd them sigh. When will they reassemble it? "

(Anna Livia Plurabelle, p. 52.)

When one has followed Joyce through his books, this

prose does not seem the unintelligible jumble of crippled words which it apparently represents to many readers. One remembers the boy for whom the word *paralysis* had a dreadful fascination, one recalls Stephen standing at the edge of the bridge trying to analyze his pleasure in the phrase, " A day of dappled seaborne clouds " from Hugh Miller's *A Testament of the Rocks,* one thinks of the amazing linguistic excursions in *Ulysses.* When all of Joyce's work is placed together *Work in Progress* takes its position at the head of *Dubliners, A Portrait of the Artist as a Young Man* and *Ulysses,* revealing itself as writing of almost unparalleled beauty, rhythmic and mellowly colored, endlessly suggestive in its ideological content, frequently humorous, stimulating in its resourcefulness, and, above all, unmistakably branded with the unique genius of Joyce.

It commemorates the place where Joyce has paused on the way he has persistently followed for more than two decades. It has been a lonely way, a way that has lost him sympathizers and friends. Many of his admirers stopped off at the *Portrait,* most of the remainder refused to go farther than *Ulysses.* A few, a very few, have accompanied him the entire distance and, even if not always understanding, have recognized the immensity of his undertaking and have been eager to overcome its difficulties. Be that as it may, neither silence nor attack has deterred Joyce from allowing his natural development to continue to its logical conclusion, however solitary the destination might prove.

He has been opposed mostly because of the unfamiliar text which his verbal innovations formed, few of his readers looking far enough past this preliminary barrier to see that the revolutionary word scheme was demanded by the vast multiple plan of the book. It was assumed that Joyce had taken it upon himself to offer the English-speaking world a remodelled version of its language. His writing was impatiently labelled as meaningless and without form, and his critics declared in effect that, far from being Stephen's ideal of " lucid, supple, periodic prose ", it was neither lucid nor periodic — and, for that matter, could only by courtesy be classified as prose.

All this is the unjust act of judging a book by its jacket. It is quite possible that many of the words composed by Joyce (always with sound philological authority) will eventually find a place in our speech, or at least in our literary language ; but such an eventuality, unless I am greatly mistaken, is incidental to the purposes of *Work in Progress*. Suppose, however, that Joyce *did* have the presumption to contribute a few suggestions for the further expansion of our language — why should the gesture be received with indignation ? English is a notorious borrower and manufacturer. Contrary to the claims of the purists it is not selfsufficient nor has it reached its saturation point, as is continually being proved by the adoption or coining of such words as *kiosk, camouflage, jitney, skyscraper, radio, jazz, kodak.* Like all other modern languages, too, it contains numerous subsidiary vocabularies evolved within the past few generations to fulfill the needs of such specialized branches of human activity as the sciences, the trades and the professions. Why, then, should it be considered an outrage that Joyce has created a terminology of his own to express a conception that lacks the appropriate symbols in the existing tongue ? In many cases he has crossed common ground in his work, and his passage has more than once left words that are full of interest. Although its length would prevent its general use, I can think of no more completely descriptive word for a skyscraper that *hierarchitectıtoploftical* nor one that blends a dozen words into a fuller summary of a man's character than *violer d'amores*, while a delight to be found on almost every page of *Work in Progress* is the pertinent humor of such words as *shampain* applied to a morning-after headache; *clapplause*, which instantly revivifies a lacklustre term, or *dontelleries*, which, referring to lingerie, surprisingly transforms the French word for lace.

To call this work meaningless and formless is an understandable mistake; but it is amazing that so few critics should have remarked its rhythmical qualities and the multitude of rhetorical devices it contains. Beside being crammed to bursting with meaning, it maintains a rhythm that accompanies the subject throughout, and if its lucidity is that of a deep pool rather than of a wash basin, its submission to discipline is no less rigorous than the classics. Consider, for example, a passage which, curiously enough, has been quoted as an illustration of Joyce's inefficiency in handling language :

" She was just a young thin pale soft shy slim slip of a thing then, sauntering, by silvamoonlake and he was a heavy trudging lurching lieabroad of a Curraghman, making his hay for whose sun to shine on, as tough as the oaktrees (peats be with them !) used to rustle that time down by the dykes of killing Kildare, for forstfellfoss with a plash across her. "

Here is a sentence that is pool-like in its lucidity, that is supple and periodic. Few authors ever wrote a sentence with a more complete consciousness of every effect they wished to obtain or with a more telling employment of the rhetorical devices at their disposal. In it the female and male characters take the form of a stream and a tree, and the development of the stream to a lake and then to a cascade through the intervention of the tree is related simply through the triple agency of verbal significance, rhythm and phonetic value.

The sentence opens, it will be noticed, with fifteen one-syllable words, the first eleven being accented, the twelfth and thirteenth hastening the rhythm through their lack of accent and the final two returning to long beats. Through this Joyce suggests the weakness and uncertainty of the stream at its commencement (girlhood). Then comes the stronger three-syllable word *sauntering*, indicating development (adolescence) and leading by a short beat to the epitritus *silvamoonlake*, signifying full growth (maturity), the further associations with the latter stage being sylvan and the silver moon reflected in the lake. The male symbol is immediately introduced in the three ponderous trochees *heavy trudging lurching*, continuing to the molossus *forstfellfoss*, which balances *silvamoonlake* and suggests *first, forest, fell* and *waterfall*, the *foss* coming from the Scandinavian designation of waterfall. The latter part of the sentence, then, completes the introduction of the two symbols by describing the creation of the first cascade through the falling of the tree across the stream.

The principle of Joyce's word scheme is valid, as I have tried briefly to demonstrate, for his vocabulary is an organic part of the work and each word, whether it be in its natural state or re-formed, has its purpose. At the same time, it cannot be denied that, as an English writer recently said, Joyce has disregarded the limited time and intelligence of common men. He has drawn from an erudition that can be communicated in its entirety to only a few scholars, especially as his interests are so diversified. In addition to this, he has sealed up many parts of the work to even the erudite reader through the unamplified allusion to subjects familiar only to himself or a limited number of people.

But this is a detail which does not seriously interfere with the literary value of *Work in Progress*. The medium of language remains at its best far from perfect, and it is seldom that even a simple short story conveys the writer's ideas in all their shades to the reader's mind. The merit of a work of art cannot be estimated solely in relation to the extent of its communication : that would be to consider artistic value as acquired instead of intrinsic. No one who has read the *Portrait* or *Ulysses* can doubt that Joyce is a writer of extraordinary talents. If his latest work presents titanic difficulties it is because of the reader's insufficient equipment rather than because Joyce has turned to writing gibberish.

And his latest book *can* be followed in its large lines by any intelligent reader. Its labyrinths of words and ideas and pictures become gradually less involved as one reads and rereads the opulent text. It opens up continuously, presenting new beauties and new wonders. The treasures subtly buried in it offer ample rewards for the efforts spent in reaching them.

It is possible that some day, when the book has been completed and given a title, that it will be edited with columns of footnotes prepared by industrious pedants after years of research. I hope not, for one of the beauties of *Work in Progress* is its mystery and its inexhaustible promise of new revelations. Like the great books of all times, it will always have different meanings for different readers. To some its grandeur will be in its mixture of legend, fact and myth, for others its chief interest will be a technical one, others will find delight in its verbal and rhythmic qualities, others will be moved by its cosmic comedy and tragedy, and for still others its attraction will lie in its boundless humor. But to everyone it should represent a cyclopean picture of humanity and the gods as viewed across the aeons that the world has whirled its people through space and the gods have given evidence of their indulgence and wrath.

———————

A POINT FOR AMERICAN CRITICISM

BY

WILLIAM CARLOS WILLIAMS

A POINT FOR AMERICAN CRITICISM

BY

William Carlos Williams.

It is regrettable that Rebecca West's article in *The Book-man,* New York, for September should have appeared in the United States. It puts both James Joyce and ourselves in a bad light.

It begins with relish — carefully defined to remove false implications. It is Paris, there is a pigeon bridging the *rue de l'Odéon,* Rebecca West has found two lines of a double quatrain in a book of Joyce's — *Pomes Penyeach* — which she has come from purchasing. " Suspicions had been confirmed. What was cloudy was now solid. In those eight lines he had ceased to belong to that vast army of our enemies, the facts we do not comprehend ; he had passed over and become one of our friends, one of those who have yielded up an account of their nature, who do not keep back a secret which one day may act like a bomb on each theory of the universe that we have built for our defence. "

" For really, I reflected... Mr. James Joyce is a great man who is entirely without taste. "

She enters then upon a long account of a game of *boules* played upon a highway in Provence to the constant interruption of passing vehicles, its points like those scored by the sentimental artist. *Shock*. Finishing with an image of a great umbrella-pine and the statement of the purpose of the non-sentimental artist, as determined and exclusive as the tree's intention of becoming a tree. Very fine. Examples: *La Princesse de Clèves*, *Adolphe*... She speaks of the bad example of Mr. Arnold Bennett's *The Pretty Lady*, of Katherine Mansfield's weaknesses, the sentimentality of Charles Dickens, implying at the same time the non-sentimental successes of Tchekov. She compares the content of the younger American expressionist writers to that of *East Lynn*.

She states that, " Seduced by the use of a heterodox technique Joyce believes himself to be a wholly emancipated writer ". Quite untrue. This is one of her characteristic pronouncements.

" But the sentimental artist (Joyce) is becoming nothing. "

She criticises the drawing of Stephen Dedalus, " He rolls his, eyes, he wobbles on his base with suffering, like a Guido Reni... a consequence of Mr. Joyce's sentimental habit of using his writing as a means for gratifying certain compulsions under which he labors, without making the first effort towards lifting them over the threshold that divides life from art ". She objects to his use of obscene words on the same grounds.

" There is working here a narcissism, a compulsion to make a self-image with an eye to the approval of others. "

" This is not to say that he does not write beautiful prose. " She refers to the scene of the young men bathing, in the early part of *Ulysses*, and to the evocations of Marion Bloom, " the great mother ". " But that does not alter the fact that James Joyce is safe only when he stays within tradition ", a path prepared by Latin Poetry.

Following are detailed descriptions of Joyce's short stories :

A Sad Case and *The Dead,* from *Dubliners.* " These two stories alone should explain why we rank James Joyce as a major writer. " Early work.

Nevertheless, " There are two colossal finger-prints left by literary incompetence on *Ulysses* ". First, the reasonlessness of the close parallelism between Ulysses and the *Odyssey* which Rebecca West finds execrable, since the theme of *Ulysses* is essentially Manichaean and opposed to everything that is Greek. She asks, in effect, what the devil is served by these analogies ? But, Bloom being in Ireland a wanderer as Odysseus was a wanderer — she quite forgets that ten lines further on she herself answers herself as to the appropriateness of the parallel : " When one looks at the works of art recovered from the city of Khochu, which are our first intimations of what Manichaeism, functioning as orthodoxy, produced other than what we have gleaned from the report of its enemies, one is amazed by the way that though the externals of Greek are faithfully borrowed and respectfully superimposed on more Oriental forms, the admission that there is a fundamental disharmony in nature causes it to create effects totally different from anything which we could possibly experience on account of Greek Art. " And why not ? Could anything be more illuminating than such a contrast ? Could Joyce have chosen a better way to say exactly what he means ?

The other " colossal finger print " occurs in the scene in the Lying-In Hospital : " The imitations of Bunyan and Sterne, completely disprove all that is alleged concerning the quality of Stephen's mind... even allowing for the increasing cloudiness of drunkenness. " Possibly. But think of the " colossal " slip of Ibsen in the First Scene, Act Four of *Peer Gynt*, the Frenchman, the Englishman, the German and the Swede on the Southwest Coast of Morocco, as dull a piece of bullyragging as one could find anywhere in a work of genius. To speak of " colossal incompetence" over lapses of this sort — one need note only the word " colossal ".

Now for line after line she goes on proving that sentences originate before words. It is a pretty exposition. She brings in cats, wild animals and babies. But what in God's name it has to do with any intention Joyce has had, not even after three full paragraphs totalling a page of double columns and small print, is she able to make clear; any relation, that is, beyond her own, erroneous, intolerant assumption of Joyce's purpose.

In this way, she makes her points, some of them valid, some not so good. I have not attempted to sum them all. She goes at the work with a will and an enviable ability for exposition. But all she says must be thrown out of account as beside the question.

Here is the very thing most- inimical to all that is forward looking in literature, going to pieces of its own fragility, English criticism in a moment of over-extension come all loose underneath. Here it is proving itself inadequate to hold a really first-rate modern moment, hanging as it must still be with gross imperfections.

I saw Rebecca West straining toward some insistence she could not quite achieve so that she appeared wholly off balance. The evidences of exaggeration and nervousness are in such things as the exhilaration at the start, the suspiciously lyric dove, the bold but unsupported pronouncements recurring through the text. But especially it appeared in the initial step of the logic, the stress upon the two lines of the little poem which would cast a searchlight of significance over all that goes before and comes after them. " The most stupendous ", " colossal ", etc., etc. There is the table-pounding of the " right, by Jove " attitude, the ex-cathedra " this is so ". Ending finally in the summary verdict that because of his sentimental defects Joyce must be, is, in fact, debarred from the privilege of launching a technical advance in literary form ; that he is great only as a conventional writer in a tradition, that of Latin poetry ; the rest gibberish — nonsense.

It means just that Joyce, firing from Paris has outranged English criticism completely and that R. W., with fair skill, is penning not so much an attack on Joyce — whom she tremendously admires — but a defense, a defense littered by a dire necessity to save all that she loves and represents, lest what he had done may " one day act like a bomb on each theory of the universe that we have built for our defence " : all accountable to an inadequacy of critical ressource in a respectable orthodoxy.

British criticism, like any other, is built upon the exigencies of the local literary structure and relates primarily thereto. Afterward it may turn to the appraisal of heterodox and foreign works. But if these are in nature disruptive to the first, the criticism will be found to be (first) defensive, to preserve its origins. Only when an acknowledged break has been forced upon it can any criticism mend itself in a way to go up into a more commanding position. Rebecca West is solely defensive in what she says of Joyce. Within the tradition lies " perfection ", the *Sacred Grove,* a study of Dryden. Outside is imperfection and formative chaos.

It is quite impossible for British critical orthodoxy (R. W. its spokesman) to say that Joyce's imperfections are of inconsequence, in view of something else larger. For if it (she) does so, it invalidates it's own major pretence to being an inclusive whole made up of mutually related parts. It can only say this is within, that is outside the pale.

We recognize its inviolable methods. But once having said that, we must step beyond it, to follow Joyce. It is able, it is erudite, it is ill-tempered and correct — due to its limited size and the opportunity offered thereby for measurement and thorough exploration.

Rebecca West cannot take Joyce, as a whole, into the body of English literature for fear of the destructive force of such an act. She must dodge and be clever and find fault and praise. She can only acknowledge genius and defect, she cannot acknowledge an essential relationship between the genius and the defect. She cannot say that on the basis of Joyce's effort, the defect is a consequence of the genius which, to gain way, has superseded the restrictions of the orthodox field. She cannot say that it is the break that has released the genius — and that the defects are stigmata of the break. She cannot link the two as an indissoluble whole — but she must put defect to the right, genius to the left' British criticism in the center, where it is wholly forced ; a thorough imposition.

Joyce does offend in taste. Joyce is sentimental in his handling of his material. He does deform his drawing and allow defective characterizations to creep in. But this does not at all debar him from making valid technical innovations in literary form, as R. W. must say it does. Both are due to the suddenness, the leap of a new force.

*
* *

It is all to an American just the English viewpoint, an old basis, without further capacity for extension and nearly ready to be discarded forever. Nearly.

Forward is the new. It will not be blamed. It will not

force it self into what amounts to paralyzing restrictions. It cannot be correct. It hasn't time. It has that which is beyond measurement. which renders measurement a falsification, since the energy is showing itself as recrudescent, the measurement being the aftermath of each new outburst.

Joyce has broken through and drags his defects with him, a thing English criticism cannot tolerate.

But even so, Rebecca West does not always play the game, even within her own boundaries, — it is the strain she is under. A descent to Freudian expedients of classification is in a literary discussion a mark of defeat. Here is a mixing of categories, a fault in logic — that is unimaginable in a person of orderly mind.

It has always been apparent to me that references to Freud — except as Freud — are in a literary discussion particularly out of place. But the use of Freudian arguments and classifications as critical staves is really too much. The reasons are simple. Freud like other psychologists uses the same material as literature but in another mode. To use the force of psychology in a category foreign to its devices is to betray the very essence of logic.

It must be patent that in any of the Freudian classifications a man may produce good writing. That is, it may be good or bad in any Freudian catagory. Comment if you like on Joyce's narcissism but what in the world has it to do with him as a writer ? Of course it has, as far as prestige is concerned, but not as to writing — a division which R. W. seems anxious to make when she calls him a genius. But the expedient is convenient if we want to gain a spurious (psychologic, not literary) advantage for temporal purposes.

What Joyce is saying is a literary thing. It is a literary value he is forwarding. He is a writer. Will this never be understood ? Perhaps he is fixed in his material and cannot change. It is of no consequence. The writing is, however, changing, the writing is active. It is in the writing that the power exists. Joyce is a literary man writing as he may — with as much affection from his material, his Freudian category as — Esop from his hump or Scarron from his nerves. It is stupid, it is narrow British to think to use that against him.

The thing is, they want to stay safe, they do not want to give up something, so thay enlist psychology to save them. But under it they miss the clear, actually the miraculous, benefits of literature itself. A silent flower opening out of the dung they dote on. They miss Joyce blossoming pure white above their heads. They are *literary* critics. That's what gets me.

Usually something has been disturbed, possibly outraged — so they search around, muck around in psychology for what *cause* to blame, instead of searching in the writing, in literature, for the *reason*. They shut the eyes, do nothing about the fact of the writing or cry " genius " — and avoid the issue. They forget that literature, like all other effects, by genius transcends the material, no matter what it is. That it, by itself, raises the thing that is to be observed into a rarer field. I don't give a damn what Joyce happens by the chances of his life to be writing of, any more than I care about the termination of the story of Pantagruel and the Sibyl. Shock there if you wish.

And this is the opportunity of America ! to see large, larger than England can.

An appearance of synchroneity between American and English literature has made it seem, especially at certain times, as if English criticism could overlay the American strain as it does the English. This cannot be so. The differences are epochal. Every time American strength goes into a mould modelled after the English, it is wholly wasted. There is an American criticism that applies to American literature — all too unformed to speak of positively. This American thing it is that would better fit the Irish of Joyce.

Their duty is to conserve and explain in relation to established facts — that is all. We Americans ourselves must still rely on English models. But we must not be misled. We have to realize that an English dictum on any work is, for us, only an approximation. It exists only as an analogous appraisal, as far as we are concerned, to fill a lack on our part of actual value.

A faultfinding elucidation of Joyce's work gives Rebecca West a final satisfaction. This is what is meant by the term "insular". Surrounded, limited yet intact. It is the exact counterpart of the physical characteristic of England. They have attempted freedom but achieved only extension of insularity, for the central fear remains.

With hieratical assurance Rebecca West lays down her fiats about everything, rising to a transcendental ecstasy at last and the longing for a spiritual triumph and the life onward and upward forever. She is speaking, that is, of a life nearly at its end, just as a younger culture or one at its beginning, in full vigor, wishes for a fusion of the spirit with life as it exists here on earth in mud and slime today.

Truly her conception of the Shakespearean fool, to whom she likens Joyce's mental processes, is cloacal if anything could be so, with his japes and antics which so distress her thought, in that transcendental dream in which the spirit is triumphant — somewhere else. Whereas *here* is the only place where we know the spirit to exist at all, befouled as it is by lies. Joyce she sees as a " fool " dragging down the great and the good to his own foul level, making the high spirit " prove " its earthy baseness by lowering itself to laugh at low truth. " And that is why James Joyce is treated by this age with a respect which is more than the due of his competence : why *Pomes Penyeach* had been sold to me in Sylvia Beach's bookshop as if it had been a saint's medal on the porch of Westminster Cathedral. "

But the true significance of the fool is to consolidate life, to insist on its lowness, to knit it up, to correct a certain fatuousness in the round table circle. Life is not to run off into dream but to remain one, from low to high. If you care to go so far, the fool is the premonition of the Russian Revolution, to modern revolutions in thought.

Whereas R. W.'s attitude is not noble, " an escape from the underground burrows of lust ", but is bred of a terminal process of life that is ending, since in an old society, as in an old criticism, exhaustion takes place finally. Lear's fool, however, is far from what R. W. paints his genus to be, but is full of compassion. Joyce, where he stoops low, has in him all the signs of a beginning. It is a new literature, a new world, that he is undertaking.

Rebecca West, on the other hand, has no idea at all what literature is about. She speaks of transcendental tosh, of Freud, of Beethoven's Fifth Symphony, of anything that comes into her head, but she has not yet learned — though she professes to know the difference between art and life — the sentimental and the nonsentimental — that writing is made of words. And that in just this essential Joyce is making a technical advance which she is afraid to acknowledge — that is actually cutting away all England from under her.

But Joyce *knows* — in spite of every barrier — in and out, self and world. And he is purifying. his effort (in a new work) which she calls gibberish.

Joyce is breaking with a culture older than England's when he goes into his greatest work. It is the spirit liberated to run through everything, that makes him insist on unexpurgated lines and will not brook the limitations which good taste would enforce. It is to break the limitations, not to conform to the taste that his spirit runs.

Naturally they strain to drag him back.

Here it is : he is going somewhere, they are going nowhere. They are still looking back weighing (good enough); he is going on, carrying what he needs and what he can. What good is it, as far as literature is concerned, to have observed, felt the pangs of sorrow that Joyce is recognized, even by R. W., to feel if he is doing nothing about it — as literature? As *literature*. He is a writer broken-hearted over the world (stick to literature as his chosen symbol). Broken-hearted people do not bother about the place their tears are falling or the snot of their noses. As literature, Joyce is going on like French painters by painting, to find some way out of his sorrow — by *literary* means. (Stay within the figure which R. W. cannot do.) As a writer he is trying for new means. He is looking ahead to find if there be a way, a literary way (in his chosen category) to save the world — or call it (as a figure) to save the static, worn out language.

Here Joyce has so far outstripped the criticism of Rebecca West that she seems a pervert. Here is his affinity for slang. Even if he has to lay waste the whole English structure. It is *that* the older critics smell and — they are afraid.

He is moving on relentlessly in his literary modes to find a way out. This is not an ordered advance of troops. Or it is

one place only in the attack. The whole bulk of the antago-
nist looms above him to make him small, But the effect is
tremendous.

To me Rebecca West's view seems incompatible with American appreciation, and though her observations appear
mainly true, they seem narrow, inadequate, even provincial,
certainly scared, protestant female — unsatisfactory. A little
ill-natured, a little sliding ; what might be termed typically
British and should be detected as such from the American
view, a criticism not quite legitimate, save for England where
it may be proper due to national exigencies like the dementia
of Wyndham Lewis.

*
* *

Joyce maims words. Why ? Because meanings have been
dulled, then lost, then perverted by their connotations (which
have grown over them) until their effect on the mind is no
longer what it was when they were fresh, but grows rotten as
poi — though we may get to like *poi*.

Meanings are perverted by time and chance — but kept
perverted by academic observance and intention. At worst
they are inactive and get only the static value of anything,
which retains its shape but is dead. All words, all sense of
being is gone out of them. Or trained into them by the drill
of the deadly minded. Joyce is restoring them.

Reading Joyce last night when my mind was fluid from
fatigue, my eyes bulging and painful but my spirit jubilant
following a successful termination of a fight between my two
boys I had brought to an intelligent end — subverted and
used to teach them tolerance — I saw !

Joyce has not changed his words beyond recognition.

They remain to a quick eye the same. But many of the stultifying associations of the brutalized mind (brutalized by modern futility) have been lost in his process.

The words are freed to be understood again in an original, a fresh, delightful sense.

Lucid they do become. Plain, as they have not been for a lifetime, we see them.

In summary : Rebecca West makes (is made by) a mould ; English criticism, a product of English literature. She states her case for art. It is an excellent digest but for a world panorama inadequate. She fails to fit Joyce to it. She calls him, therefore, " strange ", not realizing his compulsions which are outside of her sphere. In support of this, she builds a case against him, using Freudian and other non-literary weapons. She is clever, universal in her informational resorts. What is new left over — Joyce's true significance — his pure literary virtue — is for her " nonsense ". Of literature and its modus showing that she knows nothing. America, offering an undeveloped but wider criticism, will take this opportunity to place an appreciation of Joyce on its proper basis.

———

TWO LETTERS OF PROTEST

WRITES A COMMON READER

BY

G. V. L. SLINGSBY.

It was with considerable trepidation that I opened the pages of the new work by Mr. James Joyce. Upon finishing Ulysses it had seemed to me unlikely that a man could go much further in literature. After all Ulysses was making literature wear seven league boots and having to take considerable in its stride at that. So when I began to read this new volume, and found what seemed pages of madness I was not surprised, I was ready to believe it the madness not of the lunatic asylum but of a man whose sensibilities along certain lines have been developed far beyond those of his readers and who is therefore unintelligible to them.

I had hoped that Mr. Joyce might have brought his extremely interesting idea of presenting a character in the light of his emotions, his actions, and his stream of consciouness, to a greater perfection of handling, but I was ready to sit at his feet for any further word that the writer of Ulysses might have to say. So that my trepidation developed into definite disappointment as I tried to penetrate the maze of printing that Mr. Joyce would evidently have us regard as a serious work.

For he appears to have entirely abandoned the height of

his great argument to toy with an idea not new, but never I believe carried out to this extent, of making words serve as music and letting their sound convey a meaning quite apart from the actual specific meaning of each word. Miss Gertrude Stein has experimented along this line but up to the present she has contented herself with the quite simple madness that one can produce with already existing words. Mr. Joyce however has gone her one better and invented his own words if you can dignify them by that name.

Now there is no doubt that so far as reading words for sound is concerned we are but simple cave men with only the most elemental ideas of what might constitute rhythm, tone, and expression so it is extremely difficult for a reader in the folk tune stage of development to be faced with a literary Sacre du Printemps for full orchestra. One can but struggle. And in this case as you read on and on you have the sensation gadually increasing, of a temperature risen to meningital heights and you feel that by the end of another page you will have joined the coverlet pickers.

Whether or not a public can ever be trained to absorb this kind of thing seems to me extremely doubtful. The sort of person who will spend time in the exercise of a new set of muscles such, for instance, as for ear wagging, might be interested in developing a new set of brain or reciving cells, always supposing such cells exist.

After a few minutes of reading I tried to erase trom my consciousness the knowledge that the book bore so significant a name as that of James Joyce. I tried to put myself in the place of, say, the dentist's waiting room reader, who will bury himself in any bit of printed matter, from Archaeology to steam fitting, to escape the acute apprehension of his impending doom. After a half hours reading from that angle I came to the conclusion that I should think the book written by a clever rogue with a somewhat Rabelasian tongue in his cheek. For if one abandons the search for beauty of sound in this work one is struck by a certain significance in this method of shading off actual words and inventing others. Is Mr. Joyce's hog latin making obscenity safe for literature?

Or is he like an enormously clever little boy trying to see how far he can go with his public? Did he write this book while balancing a lamp on a whip with the other hand, or is he the Milhaud or Honegger of literature?

It is to be hoped that Mr. Joyce who is so profoundly respected and has been so ardently followed by the youth of his generation, is not turning on his current to make the animals jump instead of to shed further illumination on the paths of his real readers.

———

A LITTER

TO

Mr. James Joyce.

Dear Mister Germ's Choice,

in gutter dispear I am taking my pen toilet you know that,
being Leyde up in bad with the prewailent distemper (I opened
the window and in flew Enza), I have been reeding one half
ter one other the numboars of "transition" in witch are printed
the severeall instorments of your " Work in Progress".

You must not stink I am attempting to ridicul (de sac!)
you or to be smart, but I am so disturd by my inhumility to
onthorstand most of the impslocations constrained in your
work that (although I am by nominals dump and in fact I
consider myself not brilliantly ejewcatered but still of above
Averroëge men's tality and having maid the most of the oporto
unities I kismet) I am writing you, dear mysterre Shame's
Voice, to let you no how bed I feeloxerab out it all.

I am überzeugt that the labour involved in the composition of your work must be almost supper humane and that so
much travail from a man of your intellacked must ryeseult
in somethink very signicophant. I would only like to know
have I been so strichnine by my illnest white wresting under
my warm Coverlyette that I am as they say in my neightive

land " out of the mind gone out " and unable to combpre-
hen that which is clear or is there really in your work some
ass pecked which is Uncle Lear?

Please froggive my t'Emeritus and any inconvince that may
have been caused by this litter.

Yours veri tass

Vladimir DIXON